P9-DFB-930

Gareth Stevens Publishing
A WORLD ALMANAC EDUCATION GROUP COMPANY

**About the Author:** Kingsley Oghojafor worked as a reporter for a business magazine before becoming a freelance writer. He has since written articles for various newspapers, magazines, and websites. Oghojafor holds a Bachelor's degree in Mass Communication from the University of Maiduguri in Borno, Nigeria.

**PICTURE CREDITS**
Agence France Presse: 78, 79, 81, 82, 84
ANA Photo and Press Agency: cover, 2, 17, 23, 24, 25, 64
Art Directors & TRIP Photo Library: 3 (center), 4, 5, 20, 22 (both), 28, 35, 44 (bottom), 49, 67, 70, 74, 89
Oliver Bolch: 69
Camera Press Ltd: 39 (both), 54, 55
Camerapix: 1, 3 (top), 14, 15 (all), 27, 30, 33, 36, 37, 40, 41, 44 (top), 45, 51, 57 (bottom), 65, 66, 71, 80, 91
Getty Images/Hulton Archive: 12, 76
Chris van Houts: 29 (left)
Images of Africa Photobank: 9, 16, 26, 42, 56, 58, 59, 85
Paul Joynson-Hicks/Lauré Communications: 6, 7, 8, 18, 87
Jason Lauré/Lauré Communications: 32, 47, 83
Lonely Planet Images: 38, 43, 50, 60 (both), 61, 75
Mwanzo L. Millinga: 72, 73
Namilyango College: 62, 63
North Wind Picture Archives: 10, 11, 68
Mark Olencki: 29 (right)
Robert Pateman: 19, 21, 31, 34, 46
Still Pictures: 52
Topham Picturepoint: 13, 48, 53
U.S. Peace Corps Archive: 77
Alison Wright: 3 (bottom), 57 (top)

Digital Scanning by Superskill Graphics Pte Ltd

Written by
**KINGSLEY OGHOJAFOR**

Edited by
**SELINA KUO**

Edited in the U.S. by
**RICHARD and PAT SWETALLA**
**ALAN WACHTEL**

Designed by
**ANG LEE MING**

Picture research by
**SUSAN JANE MANUEL**

First published in North America in 2004 by
**Gareth Stevens Publishing**
A World Almanac Education Group Company
330 West Olive Street, Suite 100
Milwaukee, Wisconsin 53212 USA

Please visit our web site at
www.garethstevens.com
For a free color catalog describing
Gareth Stevens Publishing's list of
high-quality books and multimedia programs,
call 1-800-542-2595 (USA) or 1-800-387-3178 (Canada).
Gareth Stevens Publishing's fax: (414) 332-3567.


Originated and designed by
Times Editions
An imprint of Times Media Private Limited
A member of the Times Publishing Group
Times Centre, 1 New Industrial Road
Singapore 536196
http://www.timesone.com.sg/te

**Library of Congress Cataloging-in-Publication Data**
Oghojafor, Kingsley.
Uganda / Kingsley Oghojafor.
p. cm. — (Countries of the world)
Summary: An overview of the African nation of Uganda, including information on its geography, history, government, social life and customs, and relationship with North America.
Includes bibliographical references and index.
ISBN 0-8368-3112-8 (lib. bdg.)
1. Uganda—Juvenile literature. [1. Uganda.]
I. Title. II. Countries of the world (Milwaukee, Wis.)
DT433.222.O45 2004
967.61—dc22 2003060947

Printed in Singapore

1 2 3 4 5 6 7 8 9 08 07 06 05 04

# Contents

# AN OVERVIEW OF UGANDA

Uganda is a young nation with a long history. The country gained independence in 1962 from Britain, which had controlled it from about 1894. In the 1970s and early 1980s, Uganda suffered under the bloody dictatorship of Idi Amin. Since 1986, President Yoweri Museveni has worked hard to implement governmental, social, and economic reforms in Uganda. Today, Uganda is struggling to emerge from an impoverished economy and a poor health-care system. Despite its tumultuous political history, Uganda has been and continues to be a land of great natural beauty. The country is remarkably rich in animal life, which includes the endangered mountain gorilla and the famous African "big five" — lions, leopards, elephants, buffaloes, and rhinoceroses.

***Opposite*: Although conditions have greatly improved in recent years, health care in Uganda remains largely inadequate.**

***Below:* The number of Ugandan children who attend school has more than doubled since the mid-1990s, when the country's educational system was heavily reformed.**

## THE FLAG OF UGANDA

**The Ugandan flag, which was officially adopted on October 9, 1962, is divided into six equal horizontal bands. From the top, the first and fourth bands are black; the second and fifth are yellow; and the third and and sixth are red. The color black is supposed to represent the Ugandan people, while the yellow stands for the plentiful sunshine that the country receives. The color red represents the brotherhood of Ugandans. At the center of the flag is a white circle, and inside the circle is an image of a crested crane, which is the national symbol of Uganda. The crested crane is also featured in the country's coat of arms, which was adopted on September 3, 1962.**

# Geography

Located in East Africa, Uganda is bordered by Sudan to the north, Kenya to the east, Tanzania to the south, Rwanda to the southwest, and the Democratic Republic of the Congo (DRC) to the west. The country occupies an area of about 91,111 square miles (236,040 square kilometers) and is landlocked.

**MOUNTAINS OF THE MOON**

**The Ruwenzori mountain range in southwestern Uganda is sometimes referred to as the "Mountains of the Moon."**

*(A Closer Look, page 60)*

## A Large Plateau

Because Ugandan territory mostly lies on the East African Plateau, the country's interior is generally flat, with a gentle upward slope from north to south. The southern regions of Uganda's interior are slightly more elevated, at about 5,000 feet (1,524 meters) above sea level, than the northern regions, which rise to about 3,000 feet (914 m). Numerous mountains and valleys form impressive natural borders around the country's interior.

The plateau's western border is marked by the Virunga, or Mufumbiro, Mountains; the Ruwenzori Range in the Ruwenzori Mountains National Park; and the Western Rift Valley. The Virunga Mountains occupy the southwesternmost part of Uganda, and the Ruwenzori Range extends north from the Virunga Mountains. The Ruwenzori Range contains Uganda's

*Below:* **Margherita Peak, the country's highest point, is on top of Mount Stanley, which is part of the Ruwenzori Range. Because of its height, Margherita Peak is typically covered with snow and ice and hidden from view by clouds.**

*Left:* Located near the city of Jinja, the source of the Nile River is in Uganda. The Nile is the world's longest river and has been described as the "father of African rivers."

highest point, Margherita Peak, which is 16,795 feet (5,119 m) high. The Western Rift Valley consists mainly of Lake Albert and the Albert Nile and extends from the Ruwenzori Range to Uganda's border with Sudan. The Imatong Mountains, which rise to an average of about 6,000 feet (1,829 m), form part of the plateau's northern border. A series of volcanic mountains mark part of the plateau's eastern border, with some of the taller mountains in the series exceeding 9,000 feet (2,743 m) in height. The southernmost mountain in the series, Mount Elgon, is the tallest and reaches the commanding height of 14,178 feet (4,321 m). Mount Elgon was declared a national park in 1993.

## Rivers and Lakes

The Victoria Nile and the Albert Nile are Uganda's two main rivers, and they form the upper reaches of the Nile River. The Nile is the world's longest river and flows for about 4,132 miles (6,648 km) through northeastern Africa before emptying into the Mediterranean Sea. Lake Victoria, which Uganda shares with Tanzania and Kenya, is both Africa's largest lake and the source of the Victoria Nile, which begins near the city of Jinja. The Victoria Nile flows northwest across the country's central interior before emptying into Lake Albert, which is also Uganda's lowest point, at 2,037 feet (621 meters). From Lake Albert, the Albert Nile flows into Sudan near the city of Nimule.

**A COUNTRY OF GREAT LAKES**

**Although Uganda is landlocked, lakes occupy as much as 15 percent of the country's total area, or about 14,023 square miles (36,330 square km).**
*(A Closer Look, page 46)*

## A Modified Tropical Climate

Although Uganda is located near the equator, the country does not have a typically hot and humid tropical climate. Because most of Uganda rests on a plateau, its generally higher altitudes lower temperatures and reduce humidity considerably. Numerous lakes, cool breezes from the mountains, and frequent cloud cover also help to prevent Uganda from experiencing the full force of tropical heat.

Uganda can be divided into three main climatic zones — the Lake Region, the Northern Savanna, and the Southern Highlands — based on differing altitudes and amounts of rainfall. The Lake Region, which consists of the areas near Lake Victoria's shore, generally has a warmer and more humid climate. In the Northern Savanna, the climate tends to be more arid, although it remains relatively warm because it is a lowland region. The climate in the Southern Highlands is cooler and drier. In Kampala, the temperature can reach a maximum of about 97° Fahrenheit (36° Celsius) or dip to a minimum of nearly 54° F (12° C). In Kabale, the minimum temperature is about 37° F (3° C) and the maximum is 84° Fahrenheit (29° Celsius).

**RAINFALL PATTERNS**

**Uganda generally receives ample rainfall. Wet seasons occur in southern Uganda both from April to May and from October to November, while the northern wet season lasts from April to October. Mountainous areas in western Uganda and the Lake Region receive the most rain in the country, at more than 59 inches (1,500 milimeters) a year. Northeastern and the central Uganda receive less than 39 inches (991 mm) of rainfall a year.**

*Below:* Because of plentiful rainfall, much of Uganda is covered with vegetation for most of the year.

*Left:* Queen Elizabeth National Park is famous for having exceptionally diverse landscapes, which support an equally diverse selection of plant and animal species, including the African Cape buffalo.

## Plants and Animals

About 8 percent of Uganda's area was once covered with forests, most of which were located near either the Western Rift Valley or Lake Victoria. Today, Uganda's forests are in great danger because of indiscriminate logging. Previously, the country had between thirty and forty tree species that were considered exploitable. Mahogany, muzizi, nongo, satinwood, and Elgon olive are some examples of valuable woods that grow in Uganda.

Uganda's animal population is vast and diverse. Although large cats, such as lions and leopards, are rarely seen in the wild, they thrive in the country's many national parks and nature reserves. Many species of antelopes, including the Uganda kob, oryx, greater kudu, lesser kudu, and Grant's gazelle, are found in Uganda. Most of the country's antelope species inhabit the dry northeastern region. Uganda's lakes and rivers are home to many fish species, such as the tiger fish, barbel, Nile perch, and ngege, which is a freshwater species of tilapia. Hippopotamuses and crocodiles also inhabit some of the country's lakes and rivers. Uganda's westernmost regions host mainly mountain gorillas, chimpanzees, and small forest elephants, while zebras, topis, and elands tend to live in the country's northeastern and southern grasslands. Black rhinoceroses and giraffes mostly roam the country's north, while elephants and buffaloes inhabit both the north and west.

### NATIONAL PARKS AND WILDLIFE

**Uganda's national parks reflect the remarkable diversity of the country's natural environments, which include freshwater lakes, swamps, thick forests, mountain ranges, and savanna grasslands. In recent years, the Ugandan government has taken steps toward protecting and managing the country's natural environments and the wildlife that inhabit them.**
*(A Closer Look, page 64)*

### BIRDS OF UGANDA

**Remarkably rich in bird life, Uganda is home to more than one thousand bird species.**
*(A Closer Look, page 44)*

### GORILLAS AND OTHER PRIMATES

**Uganda is home to a great many primates, including the rare mountain gorilla, arguably made famous by American zoologist Dian Fossey (1932-1985).**
*(A Closer Look, page 50)*

# History

## The Rise of Buganda

In the 1300s, Bantu-speaking peoples formed several kingdoms known as the *Cwezi* (SEE-wee-ze) states, which were reorganized into the states of Buganda, Bunyoro, and Ankole in the late 1400s. From the 1500s to the 1700s, Bunyoro was the most powerful kingdom. By about 1800, Bunyoro had grown so large that its central ruler was unable to control the more remote parts of his kingdom. As Bunyoro declined, Buganda, located to the northeast of Bunyoro, began to absorb Bunyoro's territories. Buganda, which means "state of the Ganda people," became the region's dominant state in the 1800s.

**BEFORE THE KINGDOMS**

**Migrating Bantu-speaking peoples are believed to have entered the territory of present-day Uganda from the west between about 500 B.C. and A.D. 1000. The Bantu-speakers grew to dominate the regions south and west of the Victoria Nile. The peoples who settled north of the Victoria Nile tended to speak Nilotic or Sudanic languages.**

**KABAKA MUTESA I (1856–1884)**

**The people of Buganda referred to their ruler by the title of *kabaka* (KAH-baa-kah). Under the rule of Kabaka Mutesa I (*left, seated*), the state of Buganda opened up to foreign influences because of increased international trade and alliances. It was during this time that non-native religions, namely Christianity and Islam, first began to spread through Buganda. By the late 1870s and 1880s, Protestant and Roman Catholic missionaries both had sizable followings, and Islam was also drawing a significant number of converts.**

*Left:* This illustration is an artist's impression of the kabaka's palace in Buganda in 1890s, when the kingdom first came under the control and influence of the British.

**SEMEI LULAKLENZI KAKUNGULU**

A colorful character, Semei Lulaklenzi Kakungulu (1869–1928) has been described as the "first and most reknowned warrior in Uganda."

(*A Closer Look, page 68*)

## The Uganda Protectorate

In 1884, Mwanga succeeded Mutesa I as Buganda's kabaka, but he was overthrown in 1888 after trying to oust the missionaries and their followers from his kingdom. Power struggles between the three major religious groups of the land — Protestants, Roman Catholics, and Muslims — followed, and in 1889, Mwanga was restored to the throne with the help of a temporarily unified Christian community of both Protestants and Roman Catholics. That same year, Mwanga signed a treaty of protection with the Germans, but it was nullified in the following year after the Germans entered into a separate agreement with the British. In 1890, Buganda came under the control of the Imperial British East Africa Company (IBEAC). The company helped run Buganda on behalf of the British government until it ran out of money. In 1894, the British government, pressured by missionary groups and their supporters in Britain, made Buganda a protectorate. By 1896, several nearby states were also British protectorates. In 1897, Mwanga openly challenged British rule and was dethroned again. Mwanga was succeeded by his preschool son, Daudi Chwa II. By 1914, what had become known as the Uganda protectorate had fixed boundaries and a central government authority.

**THE BUGANDA AGREEMENT**

In 1899, the British government sent Sir Harry Hamilton Johnston on an official visit to Buganda. Johnston's task was to determine what kind of relationship would be best for Buganda and Britain. Johnston eventually devised the Buganda Agreement, which became the foundation for relations between Buganda and Britain for the next fifty years. Under the agreement, the British government promised to recognize the sovereignty of the Bugandan ruler as long as he remained loyal to British authority.

## British Colonial Rule

In the early 1900s, the British helped develop transportation infrastructure, consisting mainly of railway tracks, that linked Kampala and Jinja to cities of the region such as Mombasa, near the Indian Ocean, and Kisumu, near Lake Victoria. At the recommendation of the British, cotton, coffee, and sugar were the main cash crops grown at the time. Few Europeans, however, had settled in Uganda. It was the South Asian immigrants to Uganda who were driving Uganda's rapid economic growth. Although Uganda's economy was affected by World War I and the Great Depression of the 1920s and 1930s, the country recovered far quicker than its neighbors under the commercial leadership of the South Asians, who were mostly from either India or Pakistan. Also during the 1920s and 1930s, the British began to reduce Buganda's autonomy in spite of the 1900 Buganda Agreement. In 1953, the British exiled Buganda's kabaka, Mutesa II, because he opposed British policies. Although Mutesa II returned as Buganda's ruler in 1955, relations between Buganda and the rest of British-controlled Uganda had become strained.

***Left:*** **On November 1, 1951, Kabaka Mutesa II inspected the guard of honor. This grand military gesture was part of his birthday celebration.**

*Left:* Milton Obote (*second from right*), Uganda's first prime minister, swears allegiance to Queen Elizabeth II of Great Britain. In 1962, Uganda gained independence from Great Britain and became a member of the British Commonwealth.

## From Independence to Amin

Between the late 1950s and early 1960s, the African people of Uganda developed a growing thirst for self-government. At the same time, Buganda sought independence from Uganda. On October 9, 1962, Uganda gained independence from the British. Buganda and four other kingdoms each retained the rights to full internal self-government, operating as federal states within independent Uganda. Milton Obote, who was the leader of the Uganda People's Congress (UPC), one of the three main political parties at that time, became the country's first prime minister. The other two parties were the Democratic Party (DP) and the Kabaka Yekka (KY), which means "King Alone." In 1963, Kabaka Mutesa II of the KY party was made president. Power struggles between the Obote government and supporters of the Buganda monarchy strained relations within the country in the years that followed, and by 1966, Obote introduced laws that abolished Buganda's autonomy. The Ganda people forged a strong resistance, in response to which Obote sent troops led by Colonel Idi Amin into Buganda. Amin crushed the uprising and sent Mutesa II into exile in Great Britain. Ugandan government descended into greater instablity when power struggles and skirmishes became common between the country's various ethnic groups. Obote was Lango, Amin was Kakwa, and the Ugandan military was mainly Acholi. Ethnic divisions turned Amin against Obote, and Amin eventually usurped Obote's power in 1971.

**THE RISE AND FALL OF IDI AMIN**

**A career soldier, Idi Amin came to power in January 1971 after an unlawful takeover. Amin went on to rule Uganda with an iron fist as dictator and terrorized Ugandans. The country eventually collapsed under his poor governance, and he was overthrown in 1979.**

(*A Closer Look, page 66*)

## Uganda After Amin

Idi Amin left Uganda in disarray — the country's economy had collapsed, and civil unrest arising from ethnic tensions reached an all-time high. After Amin's departure, a number of Ugandans formerly living in exile in Tanzania returned to their homeland to form the Uganda National Liberation Front (UNLF). In April 1979, Yusuf Lule, the leader of UNLF and the former leader of DP, became president. Lule's presidency was short lived, and he was succeeded by Godfrey Binaisa, who was overthrown by May 1980. That same year, Milton Obote returned to Uganda and was elected president in December, after UPC won the majority of seats in parliament. The election, however, was widely believed to have been rigged. Yoweri Museveni was among those who doubted the validity of Obote's victory, and he formed a guerrilla group dedicated to opposing Obote that later grew into the National Resistance Army (NRA). Throughout Obote's second presidency, ethnic tensions between the Acholi, Ganda, and Lango peoples in particular brewed. By 1985, Obote was again overthrown, and Acholi general Tito Okello took power. Okello, however, lost power to Yoweri Museveni by 1986.

### MUSEVENI AND AFTER

**Lieutenant General Yoweri Museveni declared himself president after taking over from Okello. He then implemented sweeping reforms in Uganda. Although he met with limited success in some areas, such as reducing unemployment and inflation, Museveni's accomplishments include greater compliance with international human rights standards, internal security, and a steadier economy. In 1996, Museveni won the country's first presidential elections since he came to power in a landslide victory. He was reelected in 2001.**

*Left:* Some Ugandan rebel groups, past and present, have an unsavory reputation internationally for using child soldiers.

## Apollo Milton Obote (1924– )

Ethnically Lango, Milton Obote served not only as Uganda's prime minister, but also twice as the country's president. Obote's participation in Ugandan politics began when he was studying at Makerere College in Kampala in the late 1940s. He was expelled from the college before he completed his studies, however, because of his political activities. Obote then moved to Kenya, where he lived until 1957. After returning to Uganda, he formed the UPC, through which he led Uganda to independence in 1962. In 1966, he became Uganda's president and served in that position until 1971. He became president again in 1980 but was ousted by 1985. Since then, Obote has been living in exile in Zambia.

Milton Obote

## Yoweri Kaguta Museveni (1944– )

Museveni was born in the Mbarara district in southwestern Uganda. In 1970, he graduated from the University of Dar es Salaam in Tanzania with a degree in political science and economics. In 1971, when Idi Amin rose to power, Museveni was forced to return to Tanzania, where he started the Front for National Salvation, a group that was later instrumental in Amin's overthrow in 1979. After losing the 1980 presidential election to Obote, Museveni formed the National Resistance Movement (NRA). His leadership and efforts finally paid off in 1986. Since then, Museveni has been leading Uganda.

Yoweri Museveni

## Dr. Specioza Wandira Kazibwe (1955– )

Born in the Iganga district in southeastern Uganda, Dr. Kazibwe is revered by many Ugandans for her work in gender and human rights issues in the country. In 1994, Dr. Kazibwe became the vice president of Uganda. She was the first woman in not only Uganda, but also all of Africa to take on such a prominent position in government. Dr. Kazibwe herself became a fine example of the gender liberation and equality she had long been campaigning for. A trained medical surgeon, Dr. Kazibwe resigned from the vice presidency in 2003 to pursue a doctorate at Harvard Medical School in the United States.

Dr. Specioza Kazibwe

# Government and the Economy

## The Republic of Uganda

The Ugandan government consists of three main branches: executive, legislative, and judicial. The executive branch is led by the president, who is both the chief of state and the head of government. The president appoints the prime minister and a cabinet of lower ministers from elected members of the country's parliament. The president is popularly elected to serve a five-year term and is entitled to one reelection.

**THE RIGHT TO VOTE**

**All Ugandans aged eighteen and older are eligible to vote.**

The legislative branch consists of a unicameral parliament called the National Assembly. The National Assembly is composed of 305 members, 214 of whom are popularly elected to serve five-year terms. The remaining ninety-one seats are divided between ten ex officio members and eighty-one appointees from various groups. Ex officio members are cabinet-level ministers who are not already members of parliament. The country's

*Below:* Uganda's parliament building is located in Kampala, the country's capital city.

constitution requires that Uganda's parliament include one female representative for each district. Other groups represented in the parliament are the military with ten seats and disabled people, workers, and youth with five seats each.

The judicial branch is based on the English system of common law and consists of two main groups of courts — the High Court and the Court of Appeal. The High Court is actually the name for the country's lower courts. Judges in Uganda are appointed by the president. Judges serving the Court of Appeal must also be approved by the legislature.

## Local Government

Uganda is divided into ten provinces, which are headed by governors appointed by the president. The provinces — Busoga, Eastern, Kampala, Karamoja, Nile, North Buganda, Northern, South Buganda, Southern, and Western — are further divided into fifty-six administrative regions, which are known as districts. Each district is led by a commissioner who is appointed by the provincial governor.

**MILITARY**

**The Ugandan Peoples' Defense Force is an umbrella organization representing the country's various military branches, which include land (*above*), air, and sea forces. In 2003, more than 5.4 million men between the ages of fifteen and forty-nine were eligible for military service in Uganda. The number of Ugandan men fit for military service, however, was much lower, at about 2.9 million.**

## Economy

Agriculture is the backbone of the Ugandan economy, and the country's agricultural sector employed about 82 percent of its workforce in 1999. That same year, 13 percent of working Ugandans were employed in the service sector, while 5 percent worked in the industrial sector. Although most Ugandans work in the agricultural sector, the output of the sector is not proportionately high. In 2001, the agricultural sector contributed 43 percent of Uganda's gross domestic product (GDP), while the service sector provided about 38 percent. The country's industrial sector accounted for the remaining 19 percent. In 2001, Uganda had a workforce of about 12 million people, and more than one-third of Ugandans were living below the poverty line.

In 2000, Uganda bought the bulk of its imports, at about 41 percent, from Kenya. Uganda also imported goods from the United Kingdom, India, South Africa, and Japan. That same year, Germany, the Netherlands, and the United States were the three largest buyers of Ugandan exports, which mostly consisted of agricultural goods, such as coffee, tea, seafood, cotton, and flowers. Uganda imports include cars and other vehicles, medical supplies, petroleum, and cereals.

*Below:* **Agriculture in Uganda continues to be dominated by traditional methods, such as sorting coffee beans by hand.**

*Left:* **Bottled beer is an important consumer good produced by Uganda's industrial sector.**

## Agriculture

Most of what Ugandan farmers grow is used to feed the country's population. Food crops in Uganda include cabbages, carrots, onions, tomatoes, peppers, corn, soybeans, cassava, and plantains, which are a starchy fruit that is cooked and eaten as a staple. Other agricultural products include beef, mutton, poultry, milk, and cheeses. Coffee and cotton are the country's two most important cash crops because of their considerable export value. Other profitable export crops include tea, sugarcane, and flowers.

## Tourism

Tourism is a major contributor to the Ugandan service industry. The country's many national parks and rich animal life historically drew many tourists each year. Between the early 1960s and 1970s, tourism was the country's third-largest foreign exchange earner, after coffee and cotton exports. Tourism came to a standstill with the rise of President Idi Amin but was revived after his fall. Since the mid-1980s, the Ugandan tourist industry has steadily expanded with increased foreign investments. Sustained civil strife and instability in Uganda's neighboring countries, however, continues to prevent many tourists from visiting Uganda.

### INDUSTRY

**Uganda's industrial sector is partly an extension of the country's agricultural sector. Ugandan industry processes raw cotton, tea, coffee, and sugarcane into export-ready products. Manufacturing in Uganda is limited and produces mainly cement, metal products, and consumer goods, such as bottled beer, matches, shoes, and soap.**

# People and Lifestyle

## A Diverse People

In 2003, Uganda had a population of more than 25 million people. The country's population is relatively young, with about half aged fourteen and younger. Ugandans aged between fifteen and sixty-four make up about 47 percent of the population, while those aged sixty-five and older make up just over 2 percent. The Ugandan population is generally equally divided between men and women except for the group aged sixty-five and older, which has slightly more women than men.

Ugandans are an ethnically diverse people, with more than eighteen ethnic groups represented in the country. Baganda, which means the "Ganda people," form the largest ethnic group, at 17 percent of the country's population. The Ankole, Basoga, and Iteso peoples each make up about 8 percent of Ugandans, while the Bakiga, Lango, and Rwanda peoples make up a total of 19 percent. The Bagisu, Acholi, Lugbara, Batoro, Bunyoro, Alur, Bagwere, Bakonjo, Jopodhola, Karamojong, and Rundi are ethnic groups in Uganda that each include between 2 and 5 percent of the population. Non-African groups, including Europeans, South Asians, Jews, and Arabs, form about 1 percent of Ugandans.

*Left:* Located near Kaabong in northeastern Uganda, this village is populated by Ugandans belonging to the Karamojong ethnic group.

**REFUGEES IN UGANDA**

**Figures from the United Nations High Commissioner for Refugees (UNHCR) suggest that Uganda, in 2002, was hosting more than 178,000 refugees from nearby countries, such as Sudan, Rwanda, and the Democratic Republic of the Congo (DRC). Most of the refugees were Sudanese, who numbered more than 155,000.**

**Many Ugandans themselves have been internally displaced by civil fighting. In 2002, aggressive rebel groups caused between 40,000 and 50,000 people to enter Lira, a town in northern Uganda. Lira's population doubled overnight and suffered severe food shortages as a result.**

**KAMPALA: THE CAPITAL CITY**

**Located in southern Uganda, Kampala is the country's capital and largest city.**
*(A Closer Look, page 56)*

## Rural and Urban Life

The vast majority of Ugandans — about 85 percent — live in rural areas. Most rural Ugandans practice at least one form of agriculture, such as cultivation, livestock rearing, and cattle ranching. In central, eastern, and southern Uganda, rural houses are commonly surrounded by large plots of land, where the growing of cash crops or grazing animals can be seen. Ugandan farmers typically grow some crops and keep either a few goats or some poultry. Only wealthier farmers can afford to keep cattle, and the richest farmers keep imported breeds. Most of Uganda's cattle ranchers live in the country's north. From the mid-1970s to the late 1980s, Ugandan cattle ranchers suffered huge losses because of diseases and theft. Since then, the government has implemented restocking projects.

Uganda's urban population is divided between Kampala and other cities, such as Jinja, Mbale, Masaka, Entebbe, and Gulu. Uganda's urban centers are mostly located in the country's south, and young people make up the bulk of the country's urban population. Uganda also has a growing middle class, and their presence is evident in the suburbs of the country's cities, where good housing is common.

**_Above:_ The city of Jinja has the greatest concentration of factories in Uganda.**

**URBAN PROBLEMS**

**A significant number of urban Ugandans are unemployed. Many have come from the rural areas to look for whatever work they can find. Manual labor and service-industry jobs are the most common forms of employment. The number of street children and homeless people in the country's urban centers, however, has been steadily increasing since the mid-1990s.**

## Family Ties

Family ties are very important to Ugandans, who hold their families, including extended family members, close to their hearts. The basic Ugandan family unit is nuclear. In the rural areas, the basic family unit sometimes grows to include extended family members such as grandparents, aunts and uncles, and cousins. Polygamy is more widely accepted in rural areas.

Traditionally, men are considered the heads of their households, and they usually either worked the land or worked outside the home to support their families. Women, on the other hand, are typically homemakers who are responsible for bringing up children. Increasingly, more and more unmarried women are striving to find work outside their homes to support themselves and lead independent lives.

In the rural areas, many Ugandan women still lead lives subordinate to their husbands. They are not only expected to work in the fields and bring up children without their husbands's help, but are also unprotected by law if their husbands die or leave them. Domestic violence is a problem in Uganda.

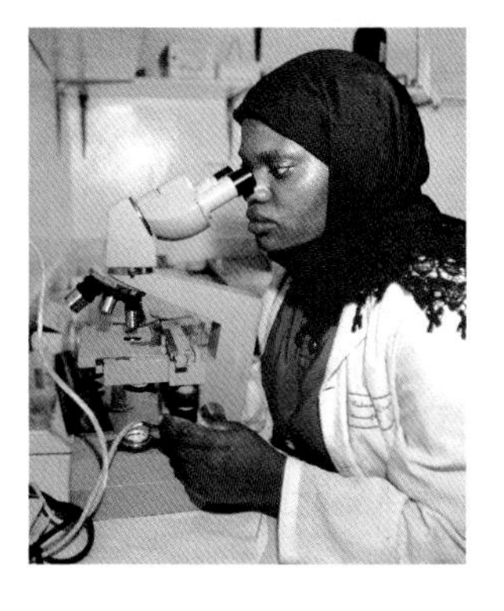

**THE WOMEN OF UGANDA**

**Although the 1995 constitution promises equal rights and opportunities for men and women, Ugandan women today generally have few rights because of the tight grip that unwritten cultural rules and traditions still have on Ugandan society. Traditional Ugandans, who are accustomed to a male-dominated society, disapprove of women pursuing careers (*above*) and gaining financial independence. In fact, the subordination of women is so much a part of Ugandan culture that some women are expected to kneel before a man to whom they are speaking.**

(*A Closer Look, page 70*)

*Left:* This Ugandan couple and their nine children live in Masaka, located in southwestern Uganda.

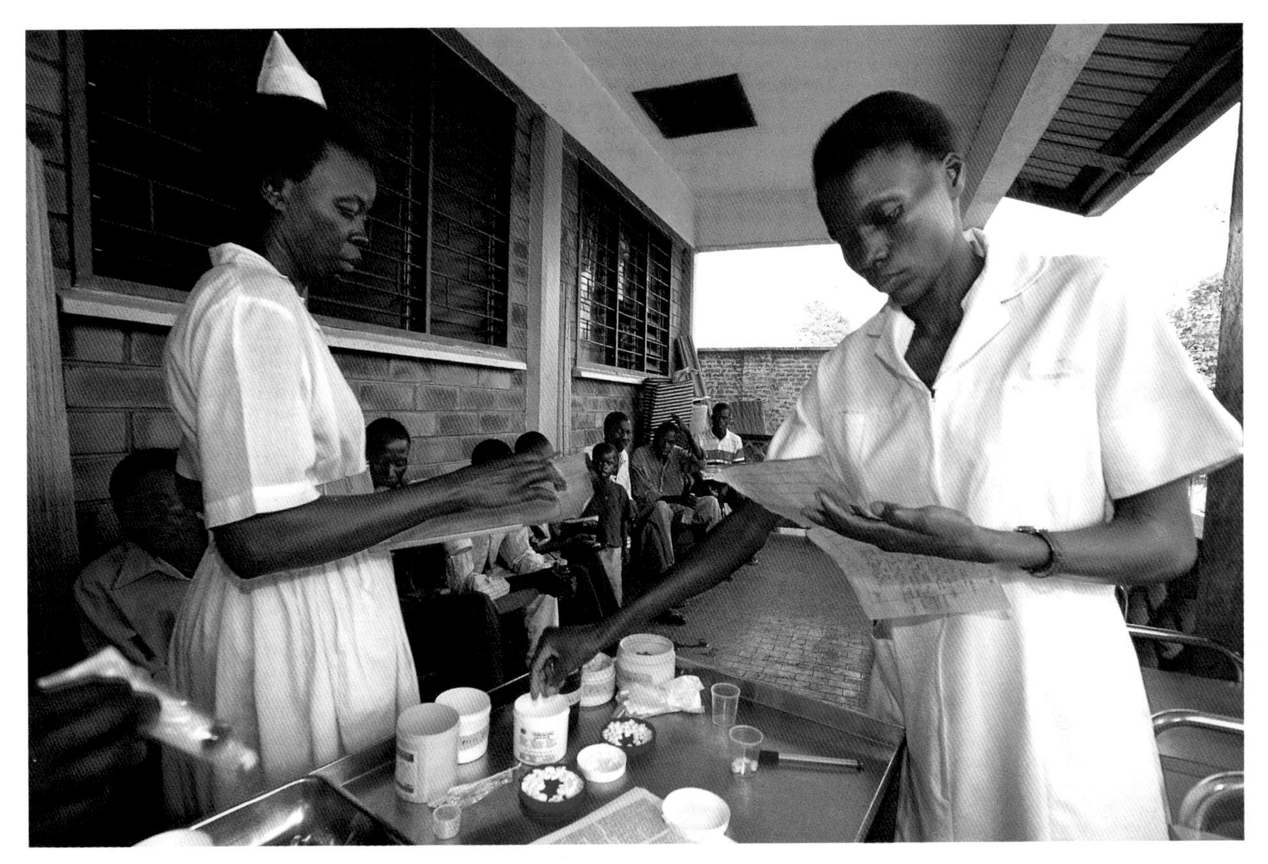

*Above:* Two nurses attend to the entire tuberculosis ward in St. Mary's Hospital, located in the district of Gulu. Diseases such as chicken pox, measles, pneumonia, tuberculosis, and typhoid, which are considered relatively easy to treat in first-world countries, remain serious problems in Uganda.

## Health in Uganda

The rate of infant mortality is high in Uganda, where as many as ninety babies die at birth for every 1,000 born. In 2002, Ugandan women were estimated to give birth to an average of between six and seven children each. Life expectancy is also generally low for Ugandans. In 2002, Ugandan men were estimated to live for an average of nearly forty-three years. Ugandan women were estimated to outlive men by about two years.

Health care in Uganda has been and still is in need of much funding and improvement. In 1986, an internationally funded program began in Uganda to improve the country's health-care facilities, help train new and existing medical staff, and provide more and better medicines and other supplies. As of 2003, Uganda had more than eighty hospitals and numerous health centers scattered throughout the country, but only about half of Ugandans had access to these facilities.

The lack of clean water in many parts of the country also makes the work of health-care providers that much harder. In 1995, clean water was available to only about half of Ugandans.

**HIV/AIDS IN UGANDA**

**The Ugandan battle against the spread of HIV/AIDS between the 1980s and the 1990s is a remarkable story of innovation, compassion, and strength.**

*(A Closer Look, page 52)*

## Education

In 1997, President Yoweri Museveni revolutionized education in Uganda by implementing Universal Primary Education (UPE). Under UPE, the Ugandan government provides free education for up to four children in every family, and two of the four children must be girls if the family has children of both sexes. In addition, the government has also ruled that disabled children will receive top priority when they enroll in the UPE program. Before UPE began, only about 2.5 million Ugandan children were attending school, and only about 300,000 students were taking the Primary Leaving Examinations (PLE) each year. Enrollment rates for basic education have since increased tremendously, with 6.5 million Ugandans between the ages of six and fifteen attending school by late 1999. In 2003, as a direct result of UPE, about 1 million students sat for the PLE.

Education in Uganda is divided into three main stages — primary, lower secondary, and upper secondary. Primary, or elementary, school lasts for seven years, while lower secondary, or middle school, lasts for four years. At the end of lower secondary education, students can choose to either pursue upper secondary education or enroll in a technical school to learn a trade. Upper

**LITERACY RATES**

**In 2003, nearly 70 percent of Ugandans aged fifteen and older were able to read and write. Seventy-nine percent of Ugandan men were literate as compared to 60 percent of Ugandan women.**

*Below:* **Joseph Okungu, the director of Kaapi Primary School, is surrounded by the students of his school.**

*Left:* Makerere University in Kampala began as the Uganda Government Technical School, which was founded in 1922. In 1963, the technical school became Makerere College, one of three institutions that formed the University of East Africa. In 1970, the University of East Africa closed down, and the college became Makerere University. Today, students at the university can pursue degrees in medicine, agriculture and forestry, the arts, education, technology, law, science, social sciences, and veterinary medicine.

secondary, or high, school lasts for two years, while programs in technical schools generally last for three years. Upper secondary education prepares students for entry into a university.

## Higher Learning

Ugandans can pursue post secondary education at university and non university levels. Non university courses can be pursued at such institutions as teacher-training colleges, business colleges, and technical schools.

In the 1980s, each of the country's three major religions established an institution of higher learning. These include the Protestant-affiliated Christian University of East Africa, the Roman Catholic-affiliated Uganda Martyrs University, and Mbale Islamic University. The Mbarara University of Science and Technology is a secular institution that opened during the same period.

**NAMILYANGO COLLEGE**

**An all-boys boarding school, Namilyango College was founded on March 23, 1902. Dorothy Matovu became the secondary school's first female headmistress in 2002. Gerald Muguluma succeeded Matovu and is still the headmaster of the college.**

*(A Closer Look, page 62)*

## Religion

Uganda's constitution promises that the government will not adopt a state religion. The majority of Ugandans, however, are Christian. Muslim Ugandans make up about 16 percent of the population, while followers of indigenous beliefs make up 18 percent. The Christian population in Uganda, which forms 66 percent of the population, is about equally divided between Protestants and the Roman Catholics. Some practicing Jews and Hindus also live in Uganda.

### THE MARTYRS OF UGANDA

**In the late nineteenth century, Kabaka Mwanga ordered twenty-two pages, or boy servants, to be burnt to death because they would not renounce Roman Catholicism in a show of loyalty to him. These twenty-two young men became known as the Martyrs of Uganda.**

*(A Closer Look, page 58)*

## Christianity

Christianity in Uganda dates back to the nineteenth century, when Kabaka Mutesa I first allowed missionaries into his kingdom. Missionary activity became especially widespread in southern Uganda, where the locals came to know the Roman Catholics as *bafaransa* (BUH-fuh-rahn-sah), which means "the French," and the Protestants as *bangerezza* (BUNG-guh-ree-zah), which means "the British." Relations between the two Christian groups were uneasy from the start and grew increasingly strained because of implicit political power struggles and the competition to win over more converts. The relationship between Muslims and Christians today is, in fact, friendlier than that between the Roman Catholics and the Protestants. In the 1930s, a group of Anglican missionaries began a separate movement, which the locals knew as *balokole* (BAH-loh-koh-lee), which means "born again." The movement spread throughout eastern Africa and

### THE HOLY SPIRIT MOVEMENT

**The Holy Spirit Movement began in the mid-1980s and grew to become one of the most violent rebel armies in Ugandan history. Alice Auma, an Acholi, was the movement's founder.**

*(A Closer Look, page 54)*

**Opposite:** The Kibuli Mosque in Kampala was officially opened in March 1951.

**Left:** Kampala is home to many grand Roman Catholic cathedrals, which are usually distinguished from Protestant churches by their heavily decorated exteriors. The Rubaga and the St. Peter's Roman Catholic cathedrals are two famous examples.

became the foundation for Pentacostalism in Uganda today. Other Christian denominations present in Uganda include the Seventh Day Adventist, Baptist, and Presbyterian churches.

## Islam

Islam is believed to have spread to Uganda from the countries of north Africa and also via Arab traders arriving on the East African coast in the mid-1800s. Uganda's Muslim community is a mixture of Sunnis and Shi'ites. Although the two groups are separated by belief in slightly different doctrines, they share many practices. Ugandan Muslims and Muslims elsewhere in the world, for example, fast from dawn to dusk during the holy month of Ramadan, abstain from pork and alcohol, and try to perform a pilgrimage to Mecca at least once in their lives.

## Indigenous Beliefs

Traditional African religions focus heavily on ancestral spirits, to which believers pray and make sacrifices for protection in their day-to-day lives. The respect for elders in traditional African religions is immense, and both dead and living elders are believed to be powerful. In fact, some Ugandans believe that their living elders can curse relatives with illnesses and other misfortunes. In southern Uganda, the Bantu-speaking peoples also recognize a God called *Ntu* (UN-too) or *Muntu* (MOON-too).

### ISLAM AND POLITICS

**Although President Idi Amin was a Muslim, his policies did little to improve the unfavorable image non-Muslim Ugandans had of Islam. In 1972, Amin ordered all South Asians to leave the country, and the move greatly reduced Uganda's Muslim population. Amin's brutal regime also led to much hostility toward Muslim Ugandans following his overthrow in 1979. President Yusuf Lule, who served very briefly in 1979, was also a Muslim, and he helped reduce the ill feelings non-Muslim Ugandans had toward Islam and its followers. In 1989, President Yoweri Museveni ordered the nation to stop discrimination against Muslim Ugandans.**

# Language and Literature

## English and Native Languages

English is Uganda's official language, but only about 1 million Ugandans speak it fluently. English is the language of instruction in schools and the language used in government. Newspapers mostly report in English, and some radio programs are in English. Uganda, however, also has its own brand of pidgin English, or simplified English that is used for communication between people who speak different languages.

The majority of Ugandans speak at least one of forty native languages. Ganda, or Luganda, which is the language of the Ganda people, is spoken by about 3 million Ugandans. Chiga, Nyankore, and Soga are native languages with more than 1 million speakers each, while Acholi, Aringa, Lango, Masaba, Rwanda, and Teso each have between 500,000 and 1 million speakers. About 5,000 Ugandans speak Soo and about 2,000 speak Ik, both of which are among the least spoken languages in Uganda.

### UGANDAN RADIO

**Many Ugandans speak or can understand several languages. Radio programs in Uganda, for that reason, can be produced in a wide variety of languages. Radio Uganda, for example, has programs in English, French, and more than twenty native languages, including Ganda, Swahili, Alur, Masaba, Nyankole, Rwanda, and Soga.**

### EXTINCT LANGUAGES

**Two native languages — Nyang'i and Singa — are already extinct. Nyang'i was originally spoken in eastern Uganda. Singa was spoken on Rusinga Island, which is located in the Kenyan part of Lake Victoria today.**

*Left:* Apart from English and their own native languages, many Ugandans also speak Swahili in order to trade or conduct business with people from neighboring countries such as Kenya, Tanzania, Sudan, and Ethiopia.

*Left:* Moses Isegawa (*left*), a Ugandan Dutch citizen, and Rosa Shand (*right*), an American, are contemporary contributors to Ugandan literature.

## Ugandan Literature

Uganda has a small but growing number of locally acclaimed and internationally recognized authors. Most of these celebrated Ugandan authors are contemporary, and their works were published after the country gained independence in 1962.

Okot P'Bitek (1931-1982) was one of Uganda's most prolific and well-loved writers. His works included *Lak Tar* (1953), *Song of Lawino* (1969), *Horn of My Love* (1974), and *Hare and Hornbill* (1978). Another remarkable Ugandan author is Moses Isegawa (1963– ), who wrote the internationally applauded novel *Abyssinian Chronicles* (1998). In 1990, Isegawa moved to the Netherlands, where he lives as a Dutch citizen today. His novel was first published in Dutch in 1998 and has since been translated into numerous other languages, including Danish, French, German, Italian, Norwegian, Polish, Portuguese, and Spanish. *Abyssinian Chronicles* was published in English in 2000.

Apart from books written by Ugandans, Ugandan literature is also enriched by books written about Uganda by foreigners who once lived in Uganda. *The Last King of Scotland* (1998) by Giles Foden (1967– ) and *The Gravity of Sunlight* (2000) by Rosa Shand (1937– ) are two recent and multiple-award-winning works. Both titles were the authors' first novels.

### FOLKLORE OF THE BAGANDA

**Throughout history, the Baganda, or the Ganda people, have always been fiercely protective of their traditions and culture.**
(*A Closer Look, page 48*)

### PLAYWRIGHTS

**Because Uganda has a strong tradition in theater, many Ugandan writers of novels and poetry also have written plays. Austin Bukenya (1944– ), John Ruganda (1941– ), and Robert Serumaga (1939–1980) are a few such writers. Some of Serumaga's more famous plays include *The Elephants* (1971), *Majangwa* (1974), and *Renga Moi* (1972). Ruganda, who is frequently considered as influential as Serumaga, wrote *The Burdens* (1972), and *Black Mamba* (1973).**

# Arts

## Pottery

Ugandan pots are mostly made of clay or metal. Ugandans have many uses for pots, both large and small, in their everyday lives. Metal pots, which could be made from iron or aluminum, are usually used for cooking, while clay pots are used for storing different types of foods and beverages such as water, milk, and banana beer. In recent years, Ugandan potters have also begun to cater to the tourism market. They not only make large decorative items, such as flower pots and vases, for luxury hotels and expensive restaurants, but also mold smaller novelty items that make ideal souvenirs.

## Basketry

Banana fiber is the most commonly used weaving material in Uganda. Inexpensive, lightweight, and useful, baskets in Uganda come in all shapes, sizes, colors, and designs. At home, baskets can range in use from fruit bowls to serving trays to wall decorations. Ugandan fishers use baskets to carry the fishes they have caught, while Ugandan farmers use baskets to sift dirt particles from crops such as coffee beans or grains.

### TRADITIONAL CLOTH MAKING AND CLOTHING

**Making cloth is one of the oldest crafts known to Uganda. Historically, the traditional cloths that emerged from the north were generally made from animal skins, while the cloths that came from the south were made from tree bark. Today, cloth making in Uganda also includes fabrics made from cotton and other cultivated materials, and these cloths are often decorated with printed designs or embroidery.**

**Most Ugandans in the country's urban centers wear modern, western-style clothing. Traditional clothing, which varies from ethnic group to ethnic group, is usually worn only for special occasions. Traditional Soga men, for example, wear a long, white robe called a *kanzu* (KAHN-zoo), while women wear a *busuti* (BOO-su-tih), or a unique long dress introduced by nineteenth-century missionaries.**

**THE KASUBI TOMBS**

Located in Kasubi, Kampala, the Kasubi Tombs were declared a World Heritage Site by the United Nations Educational, Scientific, and Cultural Organization (UNESCO) in 2001. Built in 1882, the structure, with its distinctive dome roof, was originally intended to be the palace of Baganda kabakas, or kings. Two years later, the structure, which is made entirely of organic materials, was converted into a burial place for Baganda royalty.

## Architecture

Because most Ugandans live in rural areas, village architecture, which mostly consists of mud huts with thatched roofs, is the country's most common type of construction. Paintings often decorate the exterior and interior walls of Ugandan mud huts. Wealthy rural families may have houses built from bricks and cement. Uganda's urban architecture is modest.

Jinja, Uganda's second-largest city, is home to a curious group of houses. Built by South Asians formerly settled in Uganda, the houses, which are still standing today, show certain European influences, with large front rooms, numerous bedrooms, and verandas. Because Uganda's early Asian population were mostly merchants who arrived during the British colonial years, they built houses that reflected their wealth and affiliation with the British. After President Idi Amin came to power, however, nearly all of Uganda's South Asians left the country, and their family homes have since become occupied by Ugandan African families.

In the suburbs, the architecture reflects Uganda's growing middle class. Depending on income, families live in apartments of varying sizes. Some apartment complexes in Uganda have many stories, while others are all on the ground level and surround a courtyard in the center. Families living in housing developments consisting of smaller apartments usually have to share their cooking and washing facilities.

**A WONDEROUS HOUSE: THE KISINGIRI HOME**

Located in Kampala, the famously sturdy Kisingiri Home is more than 100 years old and has a colorful history.
*(A Closer Look, page 72)*

*Opposite:* **Baskets are so much a part of life in the country that every Ugandan bride almost certainly receives one among her wedding gifts. The craft of weaving is also used in the making of thatched roofs for village huts and large, flat panels that can be joined to form either a fence around a family home or a poultry pen.**

## Music

Ugandans love listening to music. Many urban Ugandans enjoy visiting discos and bars to listen and dance to the latest popular songs or dance music. Afrigo Band, a Ugandan pop group, is well-known both at home and abroad for blending traditional and popular musical styles. *Tugenda Mu Afrigo* is probably the band's most famous album. Other famous Ugandan bands include Peterson Mutebi and the Tames, Freddy Kanyike and the Rwenzoris, and Jimmy Kitumba and the Ebonies. Most Ugandans, however, prefer to listen to traditional music, and they especially enjoy the experience if a live musical performance is accompanied by traditional dance. Instruments commonly utilized in Ugandan traditional music include harps, zithers, fiddles, flutes, horns, shakers, rattles, drums, and xylophones.

The xylophone is the key instrument in Ugandan traditional music, and there are two main types — *amadinda* (AH-mah-din-dah) and *akadinda* (AH-kah-din-dah). The amadinda has fifteen or more keys, which tend to be larger in size than those of the akadinda. The akadinda usually has either ten to twenty keys. At least two people are required to play the amadinda, and each player uses both hands. The two players play the same notes one octave apart from one another. A twenty-key akadinda requires four people to play in it.

***Left:*** **A Ugandan ensemble performs for the guests at Fairway Hotel in Kampala. One of Uganda's more established hotels, Fairway Hotel opened in 1969.**

*Above:* **Ugandan group Ndere Troupe enjoys a good reputation at home and around the world for having talented dancers.**

## Dance

Ugandan traditional dances vary among the country's regions and ethnic groups. Some groups have specific dances for different occasions. The Baganda, for example, have ceremonial dances that mark events such as weddings and births. They also have dances to entertain the kabaka. Performed by both men and women, the graceful *amagunju* (AH-MAH-gun-joo) is one Baganda dance.

Informal dances performed purely for entertainment are usually lively and festive. Dances in southern Uganda generally focus on rapid waist movements, and dancers, usually women, are dressed so that most of their bodies are covered except for their waists. Dances in northern Uganda involve mostly foot, arm, and neck movements, as well as large headdresses. Dances in southwestern and northeastern Uganda often involve movements such as leaping and stomping. The Acholi, in north-central Uganda, have group dances, which encourage communal participation and a sense of identity. During these dances, hundreds of Acholi people, all of whom know the same choreographed steps, perform the same actions at the same time.

# Leisure and Festivals

## How Ugandans Relax

Because Uganda's economy is predominantly agricultural, most Ugandans have little leisure time after tending to their plots and livestock. Young Ugandans also have few leisure hours because many have to help with household chores after school. Cleaning, fetching water, and gathering firewood are some of the common chores done by Ugandan children.

Similar to other African countries, music and dancing figure prominently in the leisure activities of Ugandans, who enjoy singing and dancing as much as they enjoy watching other people perform. Many Ugandans, including children, sing when going about their daily work. On Sundays, when many Ugandans go to church, communal singing and dancing is encouraged as a form of worship. In the urban centers, Ugandans are also known to gather in community halls, where they watch musical or theatrical performances.

**MAKING THEIR OWN TOYS**

**Most Ugandan families cannot afford to buy toys for the children in the household. As a result, Ugandan children often make their own toys from discarded items, such as worn bicycle tires and scraps of wood or metal, or raw materials that are freely available. Banana fibers, for example, are often used to make soccer balls and jump ropes.**

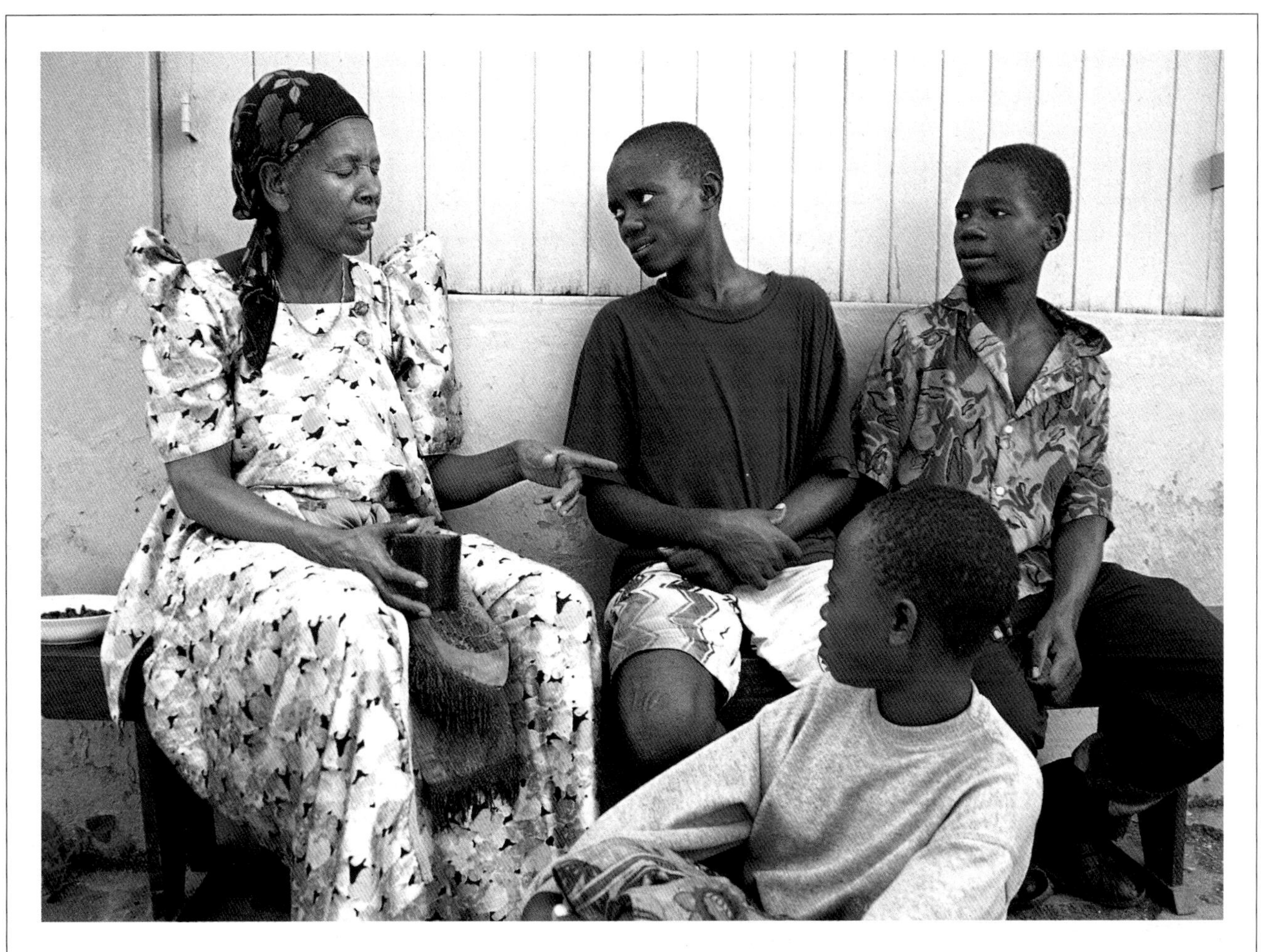

## Oral Traditions

Storytelling is one leisure activity that nearly all Ugandan children love. Storytelling is so popular, in fact, that the practice has been made part of the Ugandan school curriculum. Ugandan schoolchildren share the folktales they know with their classmates in storytelling sessions. During these sessions, the children are called to the front of the classroom to recite stories, which would have been told to them by their parents or extended family members. In urban Uganda, where television programs have been gradually replacing oral traditions, storytelling in the classroom not only entertains the children, but also helps preserve folktales well-loved by many generations of Ugandans. Favorite Ugandan folktales usually either explain features of the natural world, such as how the zebra gained its stripes or why the sun rises, or describe historical events from Uganda's British colonial or precolonial days. Other popular stories feature animals, such as gorillas, leopards, and rabbits.

*Above:* **Storytelling is an important part of Ugandan culture and family bonding. Some Ugandan folktales require the storyteller to sing a few songs. It is through storytelling that some Ugandan folk songs developed.**

*Opposite: Omweso* **(OM-wee-soh) is a favorite board game in Uganda. The board has thirty-two holes, and sixty-four seeds are used in the game. The aim of omweso is to capture as many of the opponent's seeds as possible through mathematical skill and strategy.**

## Sports

Ugandans love and play many types of sports, including soccer, cricket, rugby, tennis, squash, boxing, and wrestling. Track and field events, especially those involving running, are also popular among Ugandans. In 1996, Ugandan athlete Davis Kamoga won the bronze medal for the men's 400-meter track race in the Summer Olympics held in Atlanta, Georgia. The National Stadium in Kampala is one of the largest stadiums in Africa.

Cricket was introduced to Uganda during the British colonial years, although its players at that time consisted mostly of the English and a few Indians. Ugandan participation and success in cricket reached its height in the 1960s. Although the popularity of the sport has since declined in the country, Uganda has, nevertheless, produced a handful of semiprofessional cricket stars who have shown immense potential in recent years. These stars include Kenneth Kamyuka, Lawrence Ssematimba, and Frank Nsubuga. Sam Walusimbi is regarded as the country's cricket legend. Nicknamed the "Batsman's Paradise," the Lugogo Cricket Oval is located in Kampala and was officially opened by the Queen Mother of England in the late 1950s. To this day, the oval remains reserved for major tournaments.

*Below:* **This golf course is located in Jinja. Very few Ugandans can afford to play golf, which requires not only a club membership, but also costly equipment.**

## Soccer

Most Ugandan men are passionate about soccer, and nearly all have played the game, whether in school or for recreation. Makeshift soccer fields are found throughout the country, and schoolchildren of varying ages can often be seen playing in small groups. Ugandan school teams generally play for little more than trophies and school honors. Because soccer matches are only arranged between certain schools, however, young soccer players aspiring to become professionals have to attend those schools in order to gain the opportunity to rise through the ranks to eventually reach national or international levels. Born in 1980, Tenywa "T-bone" Bonseu is one such success story. In 2003, he was playing for U.S. team Pittsburgh Riverhounds. Two of Bonseu's older brothers once played for the Ugandan national soccer team. Today, one of them, Medi, is serving as the chairman of the Ugandan Players Association (UPA). Founded in 1957, Express FC is Uganda's oldest soccer team. Fans of the team know the players by the nickname "Red Eagles." The team was one of the country's strongest in the 1960s and 1970s.

*Above:* **Soccer is probably the best-loved spectator sport in Uganda.**

## Festivals

Ugandans celebrate a combination of religious and secular festivals. The religious festivals observed are usually either Christian or Muslim, the country's two most visible religions.

Christmas is the most widely celebrated festival among Christian Ugandans, who make up about 66 percent of the population with Roman Catholics and Protestants combined. In Uganda, Christmas festivities are centered on Christmas Day (December 25) and Boxing Day (December 26). During this time, families attend church services in their best clothes, bond by spending time together, and also catch up with extended family members and friends. Adult Ugandans cherish the rare occasion of having two days away from work, while the children are happy to see their parents at home and rested. Ugandans typically celebrate Christmas with a feast of local dishes. Traditional, Western Christmas foods, such as turkey, ham, and log cakes, are rarely served. The Western traditions of gift-giving and decorating Christmas trees are also not practiced by many Ugandans.

**OTHER CHRISTIAN HOLIDAYS**

**Apart from Christmas, Christian Ugandans also observe Easter and Good Friday, as well as Martyrs' Day (June 3), which marks the day King Mwanga ordered the killing of twenty-two Ugandan Christians who refused to renounce their faith.**

*Left:* John Baptist Kaggwa (*center*), the Roman Catholic Bishop of Masaka, becomes the center of much festivity when he visits parts of Uganda that have significant Roman Catholic communities.

Muslim Ugandans celebrate festivals similar to those observed by Muslims in other parts of the world. Because the Islamic calendar is lunar, the day on which each festival falls changes from year to year. *Eid-al-Fitr* is the most widely celebrated Muslim festival in Uganda and marks the end of the holy month of Ramadan. For the month of Ramadan, Muslims around the world fast, or refrain from eating and drinking, between dawn and dusk. In Uganda, the practice of fasting is known to temporarily disrupt some businesses. Muslim-owned restaurants and eateries, for example, may be closed during the day. *Eid al-Adha,* which means "Feast of the Sacrifice," is another large Muslim festival. *Eid al-Adha* celebrates the story of Ibrahim's complete faith in God as told in the Qur'an. The story of Ibrahim is similar to the story of Abraham as told in the Old Testament.

Secular holidays celebrated by Ugandans include New Year's Day (January 1), International Women's Day (March 8), Labor Day (May 1), National Heroes's Day (June 9), and Independence Day (October 9).

**THE UDTA FESTIVAL**

**Founded in 1997, the Uganda Development Theatre Association (UDTA) organizes an annual theater festival that features performances by more than thirty groups. About 900 rural, non-professional theater groups are registered with the association, and every year the association selects thirty-six groups to be part of the festival. The UDTA festival is aimed at educating Ugandans about new and different theatrical art forms and also preserving Ugandan culture.**

*Above* and *left:*
The Royal Ascot Goat Races have become an anticipated and well-loved event in Entebbe in recent years. Held every September, the goat races are well attended by Ugandans and foreigners living in Uganda. Before the event, the fittest goats are sought from throughout the country to run in these races.

# Food

Ugandan meals are generally heavy and filling. Starchy staples are often accompanied by a stew or sauce, meats, and boiled vegetables. Ugandan stews almost always involve a type of meat, while sauces tend to be made from beans or peanuts. Few Ugandan dishes require more than salt for flavor.

## Staple Foods

Common staple foods in Uganda include *matooke* (maa-TOE-kee), or plantains, which are a type of green starchy fruit that taste like potatoes when cooked, and *ugali* (oo-GAAH-lee), which is a type of corn bread. A variety of root vegetables, such as yams, potatoes, and cassava, are also eaten as staples in Uganda. To prepare matooke, the edible part of each plantain is cut into a few pieces after the skin has been peeled off and then boiled until the pieces become soft. Once cooked, the edible parts are drained and mashed into a thick, brown paste.

To make ugali, white corn flour is first mixed with cold water to make a paste, which is added to a pot of boiling water. The mixture should then be brought to a boil, stirring it continuously

**HOW TO EAT MATOOKE**

**Ugandans generally prefer to eat with their hands. When eating matooke, Ugandans often roll bite-sized portions into balls and then push their thumbs into the centers of the balls to make bowl-like shapes. The hollowed part is usually filled with some sauce or some meat and vegetables.**

**ALCOHOLIC BEVERAGES**

**Banana beer, which is made from plantains, is known to the locals as *pombe* (POM-bee). Millet is a grain that some Ugandans grow for food, and it is also used to make an alcoholic drink called *waragi* (WAH-raa-gee).**

*Left:* Ugandans use corn in fresh, dried, or processed forms to prepare a wide variety of dishes.

*Left:* Makeshift stalls selling smoked fish or meats are commonly seen throughout Uganda.

**INSECT SNACKS**

Every November, swarms of grasshoppers fill Ugandan streets, and Ugandans in Kampala and Jinja are delighted because they get to eat a local delicacy — grasshoppers fried with onions and pepper. Ugandans are also known to enjoy termites.

so that lumps do not form. Once boiled, more corn flour is added until a thick porridge results. The porridge is then left to cool and harden before it is cut into pieces and served.

## Meat and Vegetable Dishes

Ugandans love to eat meat, and their favorite meats are goat and chicken. Beef tends to be more expensive in Uganda, and Muslim Ugandans do not eat pork. Freshwater fish, such as the Nile perch and tilapia, are familiar meals to many Ugandans. Meat dishes, such as chicken or beef stews, smoked meats or fish, and roasts, are popular among Ugandans, who also enjoy grilled or fried chicken and lamb chops. Green and leafy vegetables are often boiled in water and flavored with salt and peanuts.

*Luwombo* (lu-WOM-boh) is a favorite Ugandan dish and is usually prepared for special occasions. The dish involves steaming portions of meat that have been covered with a rich, tomato-based sauce and individually wrapped in banana leaves. The meat used could be either chicken, beef, goat, or pork, and the sauce is made from tomatoes, onions, and peanuts. An air-tight cooking device is essential to the success of the dish, and the banana leaves have to be softened over heat so that they can be folded without tearing. Often, mushrooms and cuts of smoked meats or fish are added for a richer taste.

**FOREIGN INFLUENCES**

Uganda's major cities are exposed to foods originating from different countries. Chinese stir-frys, Italian pastas and pizza, and spicy Indian curries are not foreign to the tastebuds of some urban Ugandans. Often, foreign styles of cooking are combined with local ingredients to produce tasty results. Tilapia, for example, has become a favorite pizza topping.

*Mkate mayai* (UHM-kah-tee MAH-yah-ee), which loosely translates into "bread eggs," are a popular snack in Uganda. Mkate mayai originated from Arab cooking and involves using a thin pancake to wrap some mincemeat with a raw egg cracked over it. The pancake is folded into a rectangular shape and then pan-fried.

# A CLOSER LOOK AT UGANDA

Uganda is a land where nature has provided generously and with some sharp contrasts. Uganda may be landlocked, but lakes cover more than 14,000 square miles (36,260 square km) of the country. Not far south from Lake Albert, where the country's lowest point is found, lies the Ruwenzori Range, which are more famously known as the "Mountains of the Moon." The Ruwenzori Range's taller peaks are so high up that they are permanently snowcapped and hidden by clouds. Of Uganda's ten national parks, the Queen Elizabeth National Park is known to harbor more than 600 species of birds, while the Bwindi Impenetrable National Park — named for the thick, ancient rain forests of its landscape — is home to about half the world's population of the endangered mountain gorilla.

**_Opposite:_ Two fishers inspect the day's catch while docked on the shore of Lake Mburo in southwestern Uganda. In 1982, Lake Mburo and an area extending north and northeast of it were declared a national park, called the Lake Mburo National Park.**

**_Above:_ A colorful streetside mural in Kampala features a rich collection of folk designs and drawings.**

In the 1970s, tyrannical ruler Idi Amin engineered one of the darkest periods in Ugandan history. Amin's campaign killed hundreds of thousands, while his aides ruined the country's economy with a combination of inexperience and corruption. Although Uganda's government has grown more stable under the leadership of President Yoweri Museveni, the Holy Spirit Movement and the rebel groups that have sprung from it have been a great threat to peace in Uganda.

# Birds of Uganda

## Diverse Landscapes, Diverse Bird Life

Bird life in Uganda is remarkably rich, with more than one thousand species known to inhabit the country. Uganda's geographical location on the African continent and also its diverse landscapes, which include low- and highland forests, swamps and wetlands, savannas, and arid, desertlike regions, are the main reasons the country can support such a diverse population of birds. Ornithologists and bird-watching enthusiasts are impressed by the variety of different species and subspecies that have been identified in Uganda and believe that many more have yet to be seen as of the beginning of the twenty-first century.

*Above:* **Although the shoebill stork can grow up to 4.5 feet (1.4 m) tall, experts and bird-watching enthusiasts generally agree that it is a difficult bird to spot.**

## The Rare Shoebill Stork

Nicknamed the "whale-headed stork" by some, the shoebill stork (*Balaeniceps rex*) is actually more similar to the pelican species. Shoebill storks live in swamps and wetlands, and in Uganda, they can be seen in the Murchison Falls National Park and also the Queen Elizabeth National Park. In fact, Uganda is reputed to be the country of the world in which the elusive shoebill stork is most frequently seen. The shoebill stork's favorite food is the lungfish, which is a type of hardy, eel-like fish. In Africa, lungfish can sometimes grow to 6 feet (1.8 m) long.

*Left:* **Uganda is among the few places in the world where one can see so many pelicans roosting on the same tree.**

*Left:* The gray-crowned crane was chosen as Uganda's national bird because its plumage features all three of Uganda's national colors — black, red, and yellow.

**SPECIES AND SUBSPECIES**

**Many bird species found in Uganda including storks, cranes, ibises, flamingos, herons, pelicans, egrets, pigeons, kingfishers, doves, and mousebirds, divide into numerous subspecies. Vultures found in Uganda, for example, include the palm-nut, hooded, egyptian, rüppell's griffon, African white-backed, and white-headed varieties.**

## Uganda's National Bird

Popularly known as the gray-crowned or gray-crested crane (*Balearica regulorum*), Uganda's national bird is a magnificent sight. Colorful and statuesque, gray-crowned cranes tend to live in marshes or wetlands at higher altitudes. Because they often travel in large flocks, gray-crowned cranes cause quite a stir when they take off from or land in a particular spot. More frequently, however, cranes of this species interact in pairs. They have been spotted bowing and bobbing their heads at each other, as well as performing vigorous movements resembling a dance. Some experts regard gray-crowned cranes and black-crowned cranes as subspecies of the larger crowned crane (*Balearica pavonina*) family, while other experts treat gray-crowned cranes as a separate species.

**RARE VERSUS MORE BIRDS**

**The Bwindi Impenetrable National Park is famous for being home to the majority of native birds unique to the region. The Queen Elizabeth National Park, on the other hand, is famous for the sheer number of different bird species, at more than 600, that can be spotted within the compound.**

# A Country of Great Lakes

Uganda is one of six countries that make up the Great Lakes region in eastern Africa. The other countries are the Democratic Republic of the Congo (DRC), Kenya, and Tanzania, as well as the relatively tiny nations of Burundi and Rwanda.

## Lake Albert

Located along the western border of Uganda, Lake Albert is long and narrow in shape. About half of its length falls in Ugandan territory; the other half belongs to the DRC. The lake holds some 67 cubic miles (280 cubic km) of water in an area measuring about 2,046 square miles (5,300 square km). Lake Albert has an average depth of 82 feet (25 m), and the deepest part of the lake measures 190 feet (58 m).

## Lake Edward

Lake Edward is well-known for having remarkably clear waters. Visitors have reported being able to see hippopotamuses while they are submerged in the water. Located in southwestern Uganda, Lake Edward is also split between Uganda and the DRC,

**ENVIRONMENTAL PROBLEMS IN LAKE VICTORIA**

**Water pollution has since reached crisis levels, with human and industrial waste from nearby homes and factories pouring unregulated into the lake. The lake's ecosystem has also been forever altered by human exploitation. The Nile perch (*Lates niloticus*) and the Nile tilapia (*Oreochromis niloticus*), two export fish species that have become very common in the lake, were, in fact, introduced by the British in the 1950s, when the population of negege (*Oreochromis esculentus*), a native species of tilapia, fell below export profitability from overfishing. The Nile perch, which can grow up to 6 feet (1.8 m) long and weigh about 200 pounds (90 kilograms), has caused the extinction of many native species of fish in the lake because of its large appetite.**

**Today, Lake Victoria is also fighting a hyacinth problem that first appeared in 1989. A floating, aquatic weed, hyacinth plants grow in dense patches on the lake's surface that not only block out sunlight from the living beings beneath them but also rob them of precious oxygen.**

but the DRC has a slightly larger share of the lake. Lake Edward has a surface area of about 897 square miles (2,323 square km) and a maximum depth of 367 feet (112 m). The Ugandan part has an average depth of 56 feet (17 m).

*Above:* **Queen Victoria of England inspired the name of Lake Victoria. In the mid-1800s, British explorer John Speke, who had been searching for the source of the Nile, first recorded the presence of the lake and named it after the queen.**

## Lake Victoria

Although Lake Victoria is officially shared by Uganda, Tanzania, and Kenya, Kenya's territory at the lake's northeastern tip is relatively small. About half of Lake Victoria lies within Uganda's southeastern borders. Lake Victoria is not only the world's largest tropical lake, but also the world's second-largest freshwater lake, after Lake Superior in the United States. Living up to its reputation, Lake Victoria covers an area of about 26,557 square miles (68,783 square km) and contains an estimated 660 cubic miles (2,750 cubic kilometers) of water. The lake has an average depth of 130 feet (40 m), and the deepest part of the lake is about 276 feet (84 m) below the surface. Lake Victoria is so vast that a handful of islands are located within the lake. The Sesse Islands are some of the larger islands. The lake's shoreline is a staggering 2,138 miles (3,440 km) long.

*Opposite:* **Apart from Lakes Albert, Edward, and Victoria, which are the country's three largest lakes, Uganda is also home to smaller lakes, such as George, Kyoga, Kwania, and Mburo.**

# Folklore of the Baganda

Baganda literature is rich in proverbs, riddles, and legends. This body of oral literature helps the Baganda remember and celebrate the history, culture, values, and folklore of Buganda.

*Above:* **A woman dances to the beat of drums. Dance is an important tradition for the Baganda and is used to reinforce important values such as respect for the kabaka and other people in authority.**

## Legend of Kintu, the First Man on Earth

One of the most important stories of the Baganda is the legend of Kintu, the first man on earth. One version of the story tells of how Kintu wanted to marry Nambi but needed the permission of Nambi's father, Gulu, who lived in heaven. Gulu did not approve of Kintu because Kintu did not plant crops for food but depended on cattle instead. To determine if Kintu was good enough to marry his daughter, Gulu set Kintu a test: Kintu was to pick out his own cow from a large herd.

Kintu was anxious because the cows all looked alike. A bee soon flew by and whispered into Kintu's ear that he would land on the horns of Kintu's cow. With the bee's help, Kintu correctly identified his cow and won Gulu's approval to marry Nambi. Gulu then advised the couple to hurry back to Earth and not to return for any reason because Walumbe, who represented death, was hanging around and would follow them back if he saw them.

Kintu and Nambi listened and hurried away, bringing with them some cows, a goat, a chicken, a sheep, and a plantain tree. Nambi, however, forgot the grain to feed her chicken, and she went back to get it. Walumbe saw her and followed her back to Earth. Once on Earth, Walumbe began to spread illness and death everywhere. Death continues to stalk the Earth to this day.

This story explains how the Baganda see their history and also tells of the origins of cows and crops, which are important to daily life. The legend teaches that disobedience to parents or the king results in unhappiness and death. Obedience is an extremely important virtue for the Baganda. The character of the bee in the legend of Kintu has spawned many folktales about animals. These folktales also explain important moral themes. Many of the animal folktales involve animal pairs, such as the leopard and the hare, the cat and the fowl, or the lion and the crocodile.

*Opposite:* **A statue of the current king of the Baganda, Kabaka Mutebi II, stands outside the Buganda Parliament in Mmengo, Kampala. The first kabaka of Buganda, Kato Kintu, reigned c. 1300. He took a name similar to the mythical Kintu, the first man on Earth, in order to establish the legitimacy of his reign.**

# Gorillas and Other Primates

Uganda is home to more than ten species of primates, including the endangered mountain gorilla, the common chimpanzee, and various types of monkeys, such as the red and black-and-white colobus monkeys.

*Opposite:* **The Ngamba Island Chimpanzee Sanctuary in Uganda is dedicated to helping chimpanzees that have been confiscated from illegal poachers elsewhere in the world. Ngamba Island is located about 15.5 miles (25 km) from the northwestern shore of Lake Victoria and has an area of about 100 acres (40 hectares).**

## The Mountain Gorilla

The mountain gorilla (*Gorilla gorilla beringei*) is an endangered species. In 1987, the situation was critical with less than 250 mountain gorillas in the world. Today, the population has risen to between 600 and 620, and the gorillas are about equally divided between the highland forests about 25 miles (40 km) north of the Bwindi Impenetrable National Park in southwestern Uganda and the Virunga Mountains, which lie farther south and spread over Uganda, Rwanda, and the Democratic Republic of the Congo.

*Left:* **The reproductive cycle of the mountain gorilla is similar to that of humans, in that they can mate at any time of the year. Female gorillas carry their young for eight and a half months before giving birth. Mountain gorillas usually give birth to one offspring, but incidences of twins have been recorded. Newborns remain close to their mothers for between three to four years. Female mountain gorillas mature after about ten years, while their male counterparts mature after about eleven years. Mountain gorillas are known to live for between thirty and fifty years. Because older males of the species tend to have gray hairs on their backs, mountain gorillas are also known as "silverbacks."**

The mountain gorilla shares 98 percent of the human genome, which means that the mountain gorilla is a very close relative of the human species. Male mountain gorillas are generally taller than females, which usually measure about 5 feet (1.5 m) tall, and are twice as heavy. Gentle and shy, mountain gorillas do not adapt well to life in captivity and are mainly folivorous, or leaf eating.

## The Common Chimpanzee

The common chimpanzee (*Pan troglodytes*) divides into three main subspecies, and the eastern common chimpanzee (*Pan troglodytes schweinfurthii*) is the most common in East Africa. The other two subspecies are the central common chimpanzee (*Pan troglodytes troglodytes*) and the western common chimpanzee (*Pan troglodytes verus*). The Kibale National Park in western Uganda is home to an extraordinarily diverse community of primates, which include chimpanzees and different monkeys, such as the redtail monkey, the red colobus monkey, the black-and-white colobus monkey, and the gray-cheeked mangabey. Both the eastern common chimpanzee and the gray-cheeked mangabey are omnivorous, or eat a combination of plants and animals, while both the red and the black-and-white colobus monkeys are folivorous. The redtail monkey is frugivorous, or eats mainly fruits.

### RESEARCHING MOUNTAIN GORILLAS

**Mountain gorillas first became known to human study in 1902, when a German soldier killed one in the Virunga Mountains and shipped it back to his homeland. In the 1950s, George Schaller lived in the Virunga Mountains and studied the species. His book, *The Year of the Gorilla* (1959), became the first scientific research published about the area and the gorillas that inhabited it. Probably the most famous researcher of mountain gorillas, Dian Fossey spent much of her life protecting the species and was the first human to have experienced voluntary contact from a mountain gorilla that touched her.**

# HIV/AIDS in Uganda

Uganda identified its first case of AIDS in 1982. Ten years later, some areas of Uganda reported an AIDS prevalence rate of as high as 30 percent. This meant that 30 percent of the Ugandans aged between fifteen and forty-nine in these areas were living with the HIV virus or AIDS. By the end of 2001, however, the overall prevalence for the country had fallen to about 6.5 percent. The reduction in the rate of Ugandans becoming infected with HIV each year has been hailed worldwide as a successful attempt at combating the disease. Despite these successes, Uganda had lost close to one million of its citizens to the disease by the end of 2001. These deaths have also made Uganda the country with the highest proportion of children orphaned by HIV/AIDS. In 2001, it was estimated that there were 1,050,555 Ugandans living with HIV/AIDS, a figure that includes about 105,000 Ugandan children aged below fifteen years old.

**WHAT IS HIV/AIDS?**

**HIV stands for human immunodeficiency virus. AIDS stands for acquired immunodeficiency syndrome. HIV is the virus that eventually leads to AIDS. HIV and AIDS weaken the body's defense mechanism, called the immune system. With the body's ability to fight infection reduced, HIV and AIDS sufferers eventually contract illnesses such as pneumonia, skin cancer, and other serious infections that lead to death. There is no cure for HIV and AIDS. Doctors can only prescribe medication that slows down the virus and treats the infections.**

## The Impact of HIV/AIDS on Society

HIV/AIDS has had a devastating effect on Ugandan society. The spread of HIV/AIDS was a serious problem in Uganda in the early 1980s. Many families suffered not only because one of their family members had contracted the disease, but also because they were unable to obtain medical attention or medicines. HIV and AIDS have reduced economic growth and incomes and increased

*Left:* **Ugandan schoolchildren learn about HIV/AIDS early in their education. These Ugandan schoolboys have made cards as part of their classroom project on HIV/AIDS.**

*Left:* **An HIV/AIDS counselor in Kampala displays the contents of an anti-HIV/AIDS kit. These kits contain information on how to prevent HIV infection.**

poverty. The majority of Ugandans living with HIV/AIDS are between the ages of fifteen and forty-five, the time in their lives when people are usually most economically active. Illnesses linked to HIV/AIDS, however, prevent many of them from working and supporting their families and communities. Homes in which one or more family members are infected with HIV/AIDS are poor because they spend a lot of money on medication for the sick family members. Children of HIV/AIDS-affected parents often stop going to school in order to look after their parents. HIV/AIDS thus also reduces access to education.

## Government Support

Uganda's success at combating HIV/AIDS infections is due to the strong government commitment to fighting the disease at all levels and in all areas of life. As early as 1987, the government decided to tackle the crisis. In 1992, Uganda's parliament adopted the Multisectoral Approach to the Control of AIDS (MACA). In addition, the government also set up the Uganda AIDS Commission. This commission is the main Ugandan body that coordinates the efforts of various sectors of Ugandan society to ensure that both individuals and community and political groups work together to combat HIV/AIDS. Uganda's president, Yoweri Museveni, himself has given public support to the work of the Uganda AIDS Commission.

### THE MULTISECTORAL APPROACH

**The multisectoral approach to fighting HIV/AIDS in Uganda involves the efforts of various organizations, including the Ugandan government, medical and research organizations, schools, businesses, the media, cultural groups, community organizations, religious organizations, and organizations that care for and support people living with HIV/AIDS. International agencies, including the United Nations, are also heavily involved in Uganda's fight against HIV/AIDS.**

# The Holy Spirit Movement

The Holy Spirit Movement developed at a time when lawlessness and violent civil fighting had been part of everyday Ugandan life for nearly twenty years. Ethnic tensions had intensified during this time because of relentless power struggles between military strongmen and rebel leaders belonging to different ethnic groups. After Yoweri Museveni led the National Resistance Army (NRA) to victory in 1986, Alice Auma, a member of the Acholi ethnic group that traditionally dominated northern Uganda, responded by forming a resistance rebel group that became the Holy Spirit Movement. Believing that the Museveni government had intentions to dissolve Acholi territory and traditions, she sought to spread and encourage anti-Museveni sentiments.

***Opposite:* A group of former child soldiers in Uganda are pleading in a peaceful protest for the civil fighting to stop. They are members of the Trauma Center for Children run by World Vision.**

## Lakwena — The Messenger of God

Alice Auma claimed to be a messenger of God and that God had ordered her to fight evil, which included the Museveni government. Her views combined elements of Christianity, some animistic practices, and ethnic and political loyalties, and her formula for persuasion proved to be powerful. Auma recruited

***Left:* These soldiers sitting on the back of a truck appear relaxed, giving the impression that December 31, 1998, was a peaceful day in war-torn northern Uganda.**

many members from her own Acholi people and other Luo-speaking peoples. She also welcomed experienced fighters from various armies and rebel groups previously defeated by Museveni's forces. Alice later changed her last name from "Auma" to "Lakwena," which means "messenger" in Acholi. She was mostly known, however, as just "Alice."

## Spiritual Armor

Alice convinced many of her followers that they could wear spiritual armor to protect themselves during battle. The spiritual armor was applied with cooking oil, which followers rubbed all over their bodies. The oil, Alice claimed, was holy and made their bodies bulletproof. She also told her followers that empty bottles and stones would explode like hand grenades when thrown at their opponents. An undefined but large number of people died as a result. Many survivors soon turned to using guns in addition to wearing their spiritual armor. Remarkably, Alice, who had no formal military training, led the rebel fighters to victory on several occasions. Beginning in northern Uganda, the Holy Spirit Movement moved closer and closer to Kampala until November 1987, when Alice and her followers suffered a crushing defeat near Jinja. Alice then fled to Kenya, but she was captured and imprisoned.

### JOSEPH KONY

**The Holy Spirit Movement did not end with the fall of Alice. Joseph Kony, who also claims to be a medium of God, formed an armed rebel group called Lakwena Two shortly after Alice's defeat. Lakwena Two was based in Uganda's northern district of Gulu, not far from where Alice's movement first began. In 1988, the NRA advanced into Gulu in an attempt to crush the resistance. Many locals were killed and thousands more displaced, but Lakwena Two was not defeated. In 1991, the NRA launched another attack on the group, which had been renamed the United Christian Democratic Army (UCDA). Temporarily weakened, Kony's forces regained their military might by 1994, when the UCDA was known as the Lord's Resistance Army (LRA). Despite the steady supply of arms from Sudan, the group's anti-government campaign was losing steam, with many fighters leaving the LRA. Kony then ordered the kidnapping of children to serve in the LRA. In the mid-1990s, thousands of children in northern Uganda were taken from their families and turned into either child soldiers or slaves. In March 2003, Kony announced a ceasefire, and some children have since been reunited with their families. The LRA violated the ceasefire a few days after it was called.**

# Kampala: The Capital City

Located near the shore of Lake Victoria, Kampala is the capital of Uganda. Also the country's largest city, Kampala covers an area of about 70 square miles (181 square km) and has a population of between 1 and 1.5 million people. The city is located in a district of the same name. Uganda is divided into administrative regions called districts, and the district of Kampala is further divided into five counties, which are Kampala Central, Kawempe, Makindye, Nakawa, and Rubaga.

*Opposite:* **The site chosen for the city of Kampala was spread over seven hills. Since the founding of the city, Kampala has expanded to include other nearby hills as well. Today, the original seven hills can be viewed from Summit View Kololo.**

## A Rich Architectural Heritage

Kampala is home to numerous architecturally spectacular buildings, including a Baha'i Temple, the Kasubi Tombs, the Mengo Palace, and the Namirembe Cathedral, that reflect its long and colorful history. Built in 1882, the Kasubi Tombs, which house the remains of Baganda kabakas, have been recognized by UNESCO as a World Heritage Site since 2001. First built in 1892, the Namirembe Cathedral has been destroyed and rebuilt four times. A heavy storm destroyed the first structure, while the second structure became unsafe from termite attacks on the

### WHY BAHA'I TEMPLES ARE UNIQUE

**Baha'i temples around the world share three main design characteristics. First, the temple must have a dome-shaped roof; second, the temple's structure must be composed of nine sides, each with a door; and third, the temple must be surrounded by scenic gardens or bodies of water.**

*Left:* **The Barclay's Bank in Kampala is a reminder of the country's British colonial history.**

building's wooden foundation. The third structure burnt down after being struck by lightning. Completed in 1919, the fourth structure is still standing and can seat a maximum of 1,000 people. The Baha'i Temple in Uganda is one of nine in the world and the only one in Africa. Baha'ism is a relatively new religion, and followers call their places of worship "Mother Temples." The Mother Temple of Africa, which is located just outside Kampala city on Kikaya Hill, was opened in 1961.

## Kampala Today

Since the fall of Idi Amin, Uganda has been taking slow but steady steps toward rebuilding a once near-bankrupt economy. No where in the country is the commitment to increase production and trade more apparent than in Kampala. Kampala is not only the commercial and administrative heart of Uganda, but also the country's second-largest industrial and manufacturing center, after Jinja. With tourism becoming a major source of income in recent years, world-class accommodations are becoming increasingly common in Kampala, where luxury hotels, pubs and nightclubs, and restaurants have sprung up.

***Below:*** **The Sheraton Hotel in Kampala is the country's tallest building. It has fourteen stories.**

# The Martyrs of Uganda

## From Mutesa I to Mwanga

Roman Catholicism reached the territory of Buganda in the late nineteenth century, during the reign of Kabaka Mutesa I. The first Roman Catholic missionaries that came into contact with the territory's native Bantu-speaking peoples operated under an organization called White Fathers Mission, and the missionaries began freely spreading their religion throughout the land.

The next kabaka, Kabaka Mwanga, was strongly opposed to Christianity and sought to eliminate both Roman Catholicism and Protestantism from his kingdom. In 1885, Mwanga ordered the killing of James Hannington, an Anglican missionary bishop, and the people who worked for him. This mass execution drew criticism and protest from Mwanga's chief steward, Joseph Mukasa, who was ultimately beheaded for his views.

## From Servants to Saints

Before he died, Mukasa protected a group of pages, or boy servants, who were learning about Roman Catholicism from another page, Denis Ssebuggwawo. When Mwanga found out about these religious lessons, he ordered the capture of all the

### TWENTY-TWO UGANDAN SAINTS

**The sacrifice of the twenty-two Ugandan martyrs did not go unnoticed. They were first beatified (1920) and then canonized (1964) by the pope. Today, they are remembered as: St. Achilles Kiwanuka, St. Adolphus Mukasa Ludigo, St. Ambrose Kibuka, St. Andrew Kaggwa, St. Antole Kiriggwajjo, St. Athanasius Bazzekuketta, St. Bruno Serunkuma, St. Charles Lwanga, St. Denis Ssebuggwawo, St. Gonzaga Gonza, St. Gyavira, St. James Buzabaliawo, St. Jean Marie Muzeyi, St. Joseph Mukasa, St. Kizito, St. Luke Banabakintu, St. Matthias Mulumba, St. Mugagga, St. Mukasa Kiriwawanvu, St. Mbaga-Tuzinde, St. Noe Mawaggali, and St. Pontian Ngondwe.**

**Every year, on June 3, Roman Catholic Ugandans honor the sacrifice of the martyrs. Some organize Martyrs' Day celebrations, while others make a pilgrimage to Namugongo.**

***Left:*** **Built at Namugongo — the location at which the nineteenth-century pages were burned alive — the Martyrs' Shrine is about 13 miles (21 km) to the east of Kampala.**

*Above:* **Many Roman Catholic Ugandans frequently pray at the Martyrs' Shrine. On Martyrs' Day (June 3), especially, pilgrims from throughout the country and elsewhere in the world are known to fill the shrine to pray and pay their respects.**

pages involved. Charles Lwanga, who succeeded Joseph Mukasa as chief steward, secretly baptized the pages one day before they set off for the village of Namugongo, not far from present-day Kampala city. On the journey, two pages, Athanasius Bazzekuketta and Gonzaga Gonza, were killed. The remaining pages were held for one week and then painfully executed. On June 3, 1886, eight pages — Achilles Kiwanuka, Adolphus Mukasa Ludigo, Ambrose Kibuka, Antole Kiriggwajji, Gyavira, Kiriwawanvu, Kizito, Mugagga, and Mukasa — were burned alive. One of the pages, Mbaga-Tuzinde escaped the mass execution but was beaten to death by his father. In January 1887, another page, Jean Marie Muzeyi, was beheaded.

## Other Victims

Aside from the pages, many Christians serving the Buganda kingdom in other positions also fell victim to Mwanga's anti-Christian campaign. They included soldiers, government officials, a provincial chief, and an assistant judge. Noe Mawaggali, a Roman Catholic leader, and an unknown number of Roman Catholic and Protestant missionaries were also murdered.

# Mountains of the Moon

## The Ruwenzori Mountains

The Ruwenzori Mountains, also known as the Ruwenzori Range, are the central feature of Ruwenzori Mountains National Park, which occupies about 385 square miles (998 square km) in southwestern Uganda. The Ruwenzori Range stretches for about 75 miles (120 km) along Uganda's western border and is the tallest mountain range in Africa. In the second century, Ptolemy (A.D. 127–151), a geographer, mathematician, and astronomer, saw what are thought to be the Ruwenzori Mountains and called them the "Mountains of the Moon." Ptolemy's name has since become an affectionate nickname for the Ruwenzori Range.

The Ruwenzori Range consists of six main massifs — Mount Baker, Mount Emin, Mount Gessi, Mount Luigi di Savoia, Mount Speke, and Mount Stanley. The Ruwenzori Mountains, unlike other snowcapped mountains on the African continent, are not volcanic. Their tops are often hidden from view by clouds.

***Above:*** **Looking down from Margherita Peak, the view of Alexandra Peak, the second-highest point on Mount Stanley, is breathtaking. Margherita Peak is only about 33 feet (10 m) higher than Alexandra Peak.**

***Left:*** **These two mountaineers just reached Stanley Plateau and are approaching Margherita Peak. Stanley Plateau has the highest concentration of glaciers in Africa.**

*Above:* **Today, the World Heritage Center, the World Conservation Union (IUCN), and a number of nongovernmental organizations (NGOs) are working together in a bid to maintain the Ruwenzori Mountains National Park's status as a World Heritage Site in spite of the rebels who have entered the area and the damage they have done. Ruwenzori means "rainmaker" in Bantu. Bantu-speaking peoples named the mountains after the frequent showers that characterize the region.**

## Mount Stanley and Margherita Peak

At 16,795 feet (5,119 m), Margherita Peak, which sits atop Mount Stanley, is the highest point in both the Ruwenzori Range and Uganda. Despite being part of Africa's tallest mountain range, Margherita Peak is only the third-highest point on the African continent, below Mount Kilimanjaro in Tanzania and Mount Kenya. Africa's two tallest mountains, however, are both freestanding, or independent of other mountains. Mount Kenya rises to about 17,058 feet (5,199 m) high, while Mount Kilimanjaro stands at about 19,336 feet (5,894 m).

## World Heritage

In 1994, the United Nations Educational, Scientific, and Cultural Organization (UNESCO) declared the Ruwenzori Mountains National Park a World Heritage Site. Three years later, Ugandan rebels entered the region and began an occupation that prevented conservationists from working in the national park. In 1999, the national park was placed on UNESCO's List of World Heritage in Danger.

# Namilyango College

Founded in 1902 by a group of British Roman Catholic missionaries called the Mill Hill Fathers, Namilyango College is Uganda's oldest secondary school.

## In the Course of One Hundred Years

Namilyango College began as an institution aimed at serving two purposes: to educate the sons of chiefs and to train catechists, or people who teach the Christian religion. In 1906, the college became a purely academic educational institution and was renamed "Sacred Heart Namilyango High School," although it was more widely known to the locals as just "Namilyango High School." From 1929 to 1932, when the Brothers of Christian Instruction, also known as the Kisubi Brothers, replaced the Mill Hill Fathers in the day-to-day running of the school, it was known as "St. Aloysius College." In the mid-1940s, enrollment at the college increased significantly after new dormitories were built, and in 1960, the school population increased again after the college expanded its curriculum to include preuniversity courses. Today, Namilyango College enjoys a good reputation in Uganda for producing distinguished individuals in the fields of medicine, law, politics, and academia.

**COLLEGE MOTTO**

**The original guiding principle of Namilyango College is expressed in the motto "Education for Responsibility." The school later also adopted the motto "*Nisi Dominus*," which is Latin for "Only through God," to emphasize its religious heritage.**

**_Left:_ Namilyango College attracts some of Uganda's finest students. About 1,100 students are enrolled in the college today.**

*Left:* **Namilyango College is a respected educational institution in Uganda. This image shows the school's administrative building.**

## Namilyango College Today

The college accepts only top-performing students at both lower and upper secondary, or middle and high school, levels. In Uganda, lower secondary school lasts for four years, while upper secondary school lasts for two years. Because of British colonial influence on the Ugandan education system, students today receive an Ordinary Level certificate at the end of lower secondary school and an Advanced Level certificate at the end of upper secondary school.

Namilyango College is among the most advanced and progressive of Ugandan schools, with facilities, learning programs, and extracurricular activities that far exceed those of the average Ugandan secondary school. Namilyango College, for example, was among the first three schools in the country to gain Internet access for its students. The college also encourages students to participate in cross-cultural exchanges with students in other parts of the world, such as South Africa, the United States, Canada, and Russia.

# National Parks and Wildlife

## Murchison Falls National Park

Located in northwestern Uganda, Murchison Falls National Park covers an area of about 1,482 square miles (3,838 square km) and is the country's largest national park. The namesake and highlight of the national park, Murchison Falls is where the raging waters of the Victoria Nile are squeezed through a narrow rock opening of only about 20 feet (6 m) wide before spectacularly plunging 141 feet (43 m) into a pool of water below. Murchison Falls is surrounded by savannas to the north and rain forests to the south, and the national park's diverse landscapes, in turn, support rich animal life, which includes buffaloes, chimpanzees, crocodiles, elephants, giraffes, hippopotamuses, lions, shoebill storks, and Uganda kobs. Masindi, the nearest city, is about 56 miles (90 km) south of the national park.

## Bwindi Impenetrable National Park

Located in far southwestern Uganda, the Bwindi Impenetrable National Park is characterized by intensely dense rain forests that date back to before the Ice Age. Covering an area of about 128

**UGANDA WILDLIFE AUTHORITY (UWA)**

**In 1996, the Ugandan government passed a set of laws called the Uganda Wildlife Statute. The statute combined the existing Uganda National Parks Department and the Game Department into one organization — the Uganda Wildlife Authority (UWA). Both the Uganda National Parks Department and the Game Department were established in the 1950s. Today, the UWA oversees ten national parks, ten wildlife reserves, and seven wildlife sanctuaries. The UWA also provides support and advice to the operators of thirteen community wildlife areas.**

*Left:* Many Ugandans and tourists have trekked through the Bwindi Impenetrable National Park in search of mountain gorillas.

square miles (331 square km), these ancient forests were declared a World Heritage Site by UNESCO in 1994. Located at altitudes ranging from 3,806 feet (1,160 m) to 8,554 feet (2,607 m), the Bwindi Impenetrable National Park is home to about 300 mountain gorillas — about half of the world's population of the endangered species. Ten other species of primates and about eighty more species of mammals reside in the Bwindi forests, which also boast twenty-three native species of birds. Kabale is the city nearest to the national park.

## Queen Elizabeth National Park

Located near the city of Kasese in southwestern Uganda, Queen Elizabeth National Park is the country's second-largest national park. It covers an area of about 764 square miles (1,978 square km). Established in 1952, Queen Elizabeth National Park is famous for astonishing biodiversity that is rivaled by few places in the world. Within the compound of the national park are diverse landscapes, such as savannas, rain forests, swamps, and lakes. The park's lakes include crater lakes and Lake Edward. The park's different natural environments support nearly 100 different mammals and more than 600 bird species between them.

**KIDEPO VALLEY NATIONAL PARK**

**Located at the northeastern tip of Uganda, Kidepo Valley National Park covers an area of about 557 square miles (1,442 square km). Vast savannas dominate the landscape of this national park, which is home to a remarkably diverse community of animals. Large cats, such as lions, cheetahs, and leopards, and birds ranging from ostriches to birds of prey such as pygmy falcons and Egyptian vultures, coexist with elephants, buffaloes, zebras, and giraffes (*above*), as well as various types of primates and antelopes. The striped hyena and the bat-eared fox are unique to the region.**

# The Rise and Fall of Idi Amin

Idi Amin caused a dark period in Ugandan history that is etched in the memories of many people both in Uganda and around the world today.

## A Tyrant Grows

Born in about 1925, Amin belonged to the Kakwa ethnic group that traditionally occupied northwestern Uganda. He received little education and joined the British colonial army when he turned eighteen. Under the British, he fought battles in Burma (present-day Myanmar) during World War II and in Kenya during the Mau Mau revolt (1952–1956). A commendable soldier, Amin rose through the ranks and became an officer before Uganda gained independence in 1962. Few Ugandan soldiers were promoted to the rank of officer under British rule. After independence, Amin and Milton Obote, Uganda's first president and prime minister, became close friends. Between 1966 and 1970, Amin served as chief of the army and the air force under Obote, but increasing conflicts between the two began to divide their

**THE MAN BY ANY OTHER NAME**

**Idi Amin's full name was Idi Amin Dada Oumee. He was sometimes also known as Idi Amin Dada, as made famous by the title of Barbet Schroeder's documentary about him — *General Idi Amin Dada: A Self-Portrait* (1974). Schroeder is a French filmmaker. Amin, however, also took a liking to giving himself self-congratulatory, honorary titles, the most exaggerated of which is believed to have read: "His Excellency President for Life F.M. Al Hadji Dr. Idi Amin, VC (Victoria Cross), DSO (Distinguished Service Order), MC (Military Cross), Lord of All the Beasts of the Earth and Fishes of the Sea and Conqueror of the British Empire in Africa in General and Uganda in Particular."**

*Left:* In less than a decade, Amin brought Uganda to its knees economically, politically, and socially.

*Left:* Amin (*center*) bows his head during a prayer session in Makkah, Saudi Arabia.

alliance. In January 1971, when Obote was attending a conference held in Singapore for the leaders of British Commonwealth nations, Amin seized Uganda. That same year, Amin declared himself Uganda's president and chief of its armed forces.

## Years of Terror and Decay

Idi Amin ruled Uganda from 1971 to 1979. In 1972, he expelled Uganda's population of South Asians, who traditionally controlled much of the country's commerce. Amin then appointed trusted members of his army to run the abandoned businesses. The move ultimately left Uganda's economy in ruins. On the world stage, Amin also made some radical moves. Amin was opposed to the West, especially the British and the Americans, and was unreserved with his criticism, which worked to sour diplomatic relations. A Muslim, Amin also sought to redraw political alliances on the basis of religion. He shunned Israel and turned to openly supporting the Palestinians and Libya instead. Among Ugandans, Amin encouraged discrimination and violence between ethnic groups. Amin ordered the persecution of the Acholi and Lango peoples, in particular, because he believed that they were loyal to Obote. Between 100,000 and 300,000 Ugandans were murdered during Amin's regime.

### THE END OF AMIN

**In October 1978, a resistance army consisting of Tanzanian soldiers and anti-Amin, Ugandan exiles entered Uganda. Amin was toppled by the resistance army after about six months of fighting, in April 1979. Tanzania joined in the fighting because Amin had earlier sent his troops to seize an area neighboring Uganda in Tanzania. Upon losing his seat, Amin first fled to Libya and then to Saudi Arabia, where he lived in exile until he died on August 16, 2003.**

# Semei Lulaklenzi Kakungulu

Semei Lulaklenzi Kakungulu is one of Uganda's most important historical personalities. A politician and military leader who was very knowledgeable about religion, Kakungulu played an important part in the religious wars that took place in Uganda during the late nineteenth and early twentieth centuries. He was also the founder of Uganda's tiny Jewish community.

Born in 1868 in Koki Kingdom to a family that had immigrated from Buganda, Kakungulu distinguished himself early in his life by becoming the chief of a district of Buganda when he was sixteen years old. Kakungulu fought many wars on behalf of the king of Buganda. In 1891 and 1895, he successfully fought the Muslim armies of Arab ivory and slave traders. In 1892, Kakungulu helped defeat the Catholics. He also fought the kingdoms of Bunyoro and Busoga. Kakungulu enlarged the territory of Buganda by conquering groups and tribes up to the northern border with Sudan. These important victories brought Kakungulu much power and prestige. His position was further enhanced when he married the daughter of King Mutesa I and, later, the daughter of Mutesa's son.

*Left:* **Semei Lulaklenzi Kakungulu was an excellent military leader who led Buganda to victory in many of the wars of the late nineteeth century. This illustration from his era depicts a Baganda warrior as he recounts his battle exploits to the royal court of Buganda.**

## Kakungulu and the British

The British, who at this time were expanding their influence in Uganda, realized that they needed Kakungulu and his armies to help conquer territory in East Africa. When Buganda became a British protectorate in 1894, the British authorities allowed Kakungulu to continue subduing various tribes. In return for his military help, the British made Kakungulu military governor of the eastern province of Uganda. Kakungulu, however, wanted to be king of Buganda and expected the British authorities to appoint him king because of all the military help that he had offered the British. The British, however, did not wish to appoint him king for many reasons, one of which was the fact that he was not of Baganda royal lineage. Instead, Kakungulu was made a regional chief in 1904 and put in charge of the administration of Busoga district in 1906. Kakungulu continued his efforts to get the British to appoint him king, but they refused. Kakungulu was bitterly disappointed and retired from his political and military appointments in 1913. Although he never ruled his country, Kakungulu was a major Uganda military figure without whom the British would have had much difficulty extending their political and economic influence in East Africa.

*Above:* **An Anglican priest works at his office in the Anglican Cathedral in Kampala, Uganda. Kakungulu became an Anglican in the 1880s, but grew increasingly weary of the religion due to the British authorities's refusal to appoint him king of Buganda. Kakungulu eventually converted to Judaism and founded Uganda's small Jewish community. By the time Kakungulu died in 1928, there were about two thousand Ugandans who had converted to Judaism. Today, Uganda's Jewish community numbers several hundred.**

# The Women of Uganda

## Traditional Gender Roles

Ugandan society is traditionally male-dominated. Unmarried women are taught to obey their fathers and brothers, while married women are expected to always obey their husbands. Married men are, in turn, expected to work outside the home to support and take care of their wives and children. In keeping with such cultural expectations, women in Uganda historically had few legal rights. Their lack of legal protection, however, has led to many Ugandan women today being saddled with more than their traditional share of household responsibilities. Rural women, especially, are not only homemakers and mothers, but also work tilling the family land to cultivate crops, both to eat and to sell. Furthermore, their husbands keep the money gained from the crops sold. Despite their immense workloads, few rural women can claim ownership of the land that they work on and are likely to become homeless and penniless if their marriages end in divorce or if their husbands die.

*Above* and *opposite:* **Rural Ugandans make up about 85 percent of the country's population, and women make up some 80 percent of Uganda's agricultural workforce.**

## Pursuing Gender Equality

In the late 1980s, the Museveni government announced its commitment to reduce discrimination against women in the country. Adopted in 1995, Uganda's current constitution promises gender equality in the eyes of Ugandan law and in government policies. Although the Museveni government has attempted to improve the lives of Ugandan women through the 1995 constitution, the National Gender Policy (1995), and the Ministry of Gender and Community Development, many Ugandans, both men and women, find it hard to overturn the long-standing traditions of everyday Ugandan life. The difficulties Ugandan women face in owning land, for example, remain a much debated and unresolved issue today. Many nongovernmental organizations (NGOs), such as the Women of Uganda Network (WOUGNET), have been set up in response to the gross injustices that many Ugandan women face in spite of the steps taken by the Museveni government. Critics have pointed out that the government's gender policies are good in theory but have no real effect on most women's lives.

**UGANDA COUNCIL OF WOMEN**

**From as early as 1960, Ugandan women have joined the Uganda Council of Women to campaign for laws that would protect the welfare of women in the country. The organization called for laws that gave women the right to own property and also the right to have custody of their children in the event that their marriages ended in divorce. Civil wars in the 1970s and 1980s diverted attention away from women's issues.**

A Better
Future for
Ugandans
UGANDA

# A Wonderous House: The Kisingiri Home

## The House Itself

Located in Mengo, Kampala, the legendary Kisingiri house was built on a 3-acre (1.2-hectare) plot of land in the late nineteenth century. The house has as many as seventy rooms, which are spread over three stories. The walls of the house were built from dried-mud bricks and stone, while the flooring, staircases, windows, and doors were made from wood. Dominating the interior of the house are two enormous rooms, each of which is reputedly large enough in itself to accommodate a modest house. Some of the smaller rooms measure 20 feet long by 20 feet wide (6 by 6 m). Also inside the house is a 20-foot (6-m) long swimming pool. Over the years, parts of the house were renovated in order to provide the interior of the house with electricity and running water, as well as bathtubs, sinks, and toilets.

*Below:* **Built in the late nineteenth century, the Kisingiri home features two enormous rooms and an indoor pool, which was unusual for its time.**

*Left:* **The Kisingiri estate is home to some unusual pets. Three very old tortoises are famous for gracing the Kisingiris's sprawling front lawn and enthralling visitors when they arrive. The three tortoises have been living on the compound since the mid-twentieth century, when they were brought to Uganda from Seychelles. Experts have been unable to determine the age of the tortoises, but speculations range between two and three hundred years.**

Today, the outside of the Kisingiri house is blue. Apart from the rusty metal sheets that form the sloping multitiered roof, the house is said to be in excellent condition despite being over one hundred years old. In fact, some observers have gone as far as to say that not a single crack can be found in the structure. The old-fashioned architectural style of the building is probably the only sign of its age.

## The History of the House

Construction for the Kisingiri house was ordered by Zakaria Kizito Kisingiri, who was one of three regents, or royal advisors, to young Kabaka Daudi Chwa II. Chwa II was a child when he succeeded his father, Kabaka Mwanga, who was forced out of power by the British. Because of his privileged position, Kisingiri was able to afford a large and luxurious home.

In 1917, Zakaria Kisingiri died, and his son Stanley took over as head of the household. Stanley Kisingiri married Beatrice Muggale, a stepsister of Kabaka Mutesa II. Although Stanley died in 1991, Beatrice continues to live in the Kisingiri house with their children and grandchildren. For a brief period of time, while Stanley was still studying overseas, the Kisingiri house functioned as a *gombolola* (gohm-boh-LOH-lah), or county court.

MARKET
Enjoy
Coca-Cola
Coke
Enjoy
Coca-Cola
Coke
Coca-Cola
Coke

# RELATIONS WITH NORTH AMERICA

For decades after gaining independence from Britain, Uganda did not enjoy friendly relations with most of the developed world, including North America. The harsh policies of its early leaders such as Milton Obote and Idi Amin isolated Uganda from many Western countries. Relations with neighboring African countries, including Tanzania and Rwanda, were also not friendly. Contact between Uganda and North America was, therefore, limited for much of the latter half of the twentieth century.

*Opposite:* **Many North American products, including the popular soft drink Coca-Cola, are widely available in Uganda.**

Relations between Uganda and the United States began improving, however, beginning when Yoweri Museveni became president in 1996. The United States has welcomed Uganda's renewed commitment to democracy, economic development, and human rights. Trade between North America and Uganda has also increased since the late 1990s. President Museveni has visited the United States several times and U.S. presidents Bill Clinton and George W. Bush have both visited Uganda. Many North Americans live in Uganda, working with humanitarian organizations, and a large community of Americans of Ugandan heritage helps preserve Ugandan culture in the United States.

*Above:* **This sign on the side of a building in Kampala is painted in the style of the Coca-Cola logo.**

## Historical Ties

Diplomatic relations between Uganda and the United States were first established soon after Uganda became an independent republic in 1962. Ties between the two countries at first grew steadily, particularly in the area of trade and humanitarian assistance. The U.S. government began sending Peace Corps volunteers to Uganda in 1963 to work mainly in the field of primary and secondary school education.

Relations between Uganda and many Western countries, including the United States, deteriorated when Idi Amin came to power in Uganda in January 1971. While the British government expressed serious concerns over Amin's expulsion of South Asians in 1972, the U.S. government became increasingly worried about the security of U.S. citizens living and working in Uganda. In 1973, the U.S. government withdrew Peace Corps volunteers from Uganda and ended economic assistance to the country. Later that year, the Ugandan government expelled U.S. Marines that were in charge of providing security for U.S. government property in Uganda. American embassy officials

***Below:*** **American anthropologists Martin and Osa Johnson pose with their African assistant by a railway car bound for Kampala, Uganda. The Johnsons traveled extensively in central and east Africa. In 1929, they sailed down the Nile into northern Uganda. The couple made many films of their travels, including *Congorilla* (1932), the first movie with sound shot in Africa. Today, the couple's letters, expedition reports, photgraphs, and films are all exhibited at the Martin and Osa Johnson Safari Museum in Chanute, Kansas, which was Osa's hometown.**

began receiving threats as the security situation worsened. In response, the U.S. government decided to close its embassy in Kampala. Several years later, in 1978, the U.S. government placed an embargo on all U.S. trade with Uganda, marking a low point in the relations between the two countries.

*Above:* **A U.S. Peace Corps volunteer teacher locates the North American continent on a world map during a geography lesson in a school in Kampala. The first group of Peace Corps volunteers, who arrived in Uganda in 1964, were teachers.**

## Relations in the 1980s and 1990s

A new phase in relations between Uganda and the United States started after Idi Amin fell from power in 1979. The U.S. government reopened its embassy in Kampala and began an economic aid program amounting to about U.S. $10 million dollars over the next decade. The program included humanitarian assistance in the form of food, medical supplies, and money to repair hospitals. Relations have continued improving gradually, especially since 1986, when Yoweri Museveni took charge of Uganda. The flow of economic aid from the United States to Uganda and cultural exchanges between the two countries has increased. Today, partnerships between the two countries have been forged in diverse fields, including health care, education, environmental protection, and human rights.

*Left:* **U.S. president Bill Clinton (*second from left*) walks with a group of Ugandan children during his visit to the Kisowera School near Kampala in March 1998. He is accompanied by his wife, Hillary Clinton (*back row, second from right*), and Ugandan president Museveni (*back row, right*).**

## Presidential Visits

Today, the United States and Uganda enjoy friendly and close relations. Since 1998, there have been frequent visits by U.S. and Ugandan officials to each other's countries. The heads of state of the United States and Uganda have also exchanged visits, with Bill Clinton being the first U.S. president to visit Uganda in March 1998. Clinton's visit to Uganda was part of a six-country tour of the African continent and also included trips to Ghana, South Africa, Botswana, and Senegal. Clinton spent two days in Uganda and addressed politicians and businesspeople about Uganda's economic recovery and transition towards democracy. Clinton urged President Yoweri Museveni to allow greater political freedom in Uganda, and he also promised Uganda millions of dollars in aid for education, health care, and food.

President Yoweri Museveni has visited the United States on several occasions. In June 2003, the president traveled to the United States for a six-day visit, during which he met with President George W. Bush. While in the United States, President Museveni also held discussions with senior U.S. government officials on various issues, including Uganda's relentless fight against the spread of HIV/AIDS . Museveni also encouraged U.S.

investors to invest in the growing Ugandan economy, promising them the security of their investments and sound government policies. In July 2003, President George W. Bush became the second U.S. president to visit Uganda in just over five years. President Bush's trip to Uganda was part of a five-country tour of Africa. In Uganda, President Bush took the opportunity to praise the Ugandan government's successful efforts to develop the Ugandan economy and combat the spread of HIV/AIDS.

## United in the Fight Against Terrorism

In August 1998, the United States launched air strikes against suspected terrorist targets in Sudan and Afghanistan in retaliation for the bombings of the U.S. embassies in Kenya and Tanzania earlier that month. The Ugandan government voiced public support for the U.S. action. Five days after the air strikes, bombs exploded on three Kampala buses, killing twenty-eight people. It is believed that these terrorist attacks in Kampala were in response to Uganda's support for the United States.

After the September 11 terrorist attacks on the World Trade Center and the Pentagon, Uganda pledged full cooperation with the U.S. government in its attempts bring those responsible to justice. The Ugandan government continues its strong support for the U.S.-led war against international terrorism. For its part, the United States trains some Ugandan troops as part of the African Crisis Response Initiative that addresses conflicts in Africa.

***Left:*** **U.S. president George W. Bush (*right*), U.S. first lady Laura Bush (*center*), and the president of Uganda, Yoweri Museveni (*left*), watch a performance by the Watoto Children's Choir of Uganda in June 2003, in the Rose Garden of the White House, in Washington, D.C. President Museveni was on an official visit to the United States.**

## U.S.-Uganda Economic Ties

The United States and Uganda enjoy close commercial and economic ties. Several moves made by the governments of both countries are helping to deepen this relationship. One of the important economic partnerships between the United States and Uganda has been forged under the Africa Growth Opportunity Act (AGOA). This piece of U.S. legislation, passed in 2000, gives certain countries of sub-Saharan Africa, including Uganda, access to U.S. markets. The AGOA also seeks to improve the economies of sub-Saharan countries, such as Uganda, by promoting economic reforms and giving Ugandan companies access to U.S. loans and technical knowledge.

The African Development Foundation is another initiative in which Uganda and the United States are partners. Established in 1984, the foundation has been supporting more than thirty-five economic development projects in Uganda since 1993. Projects in Uganda aim to improve the lives of rural Ugandans by providing them with money and expertise to start and run small businesses. Some examples of the work of the foundation include a project to assist Ugandans to start and run a silkworm cooperative and

***Below:*** **A Ugandan vendor sells her colorful vegetables at a Kampala market. Some North American aid agencies are involved in schemes that help women establish small businesses. The income the women earn from selling surplus crops, clothes, or crafts helps to increase the standard of living for their families.**

*Left:* **Executive director of the World Food Program (WFP) Catherine Bertini (*left*) talks to homeless and orphaned children at the Kamwokya Christian Caring Community Site in Kampala in February 2002. Bertini visited Uganda to officially open a new WFP regional bureau for eastern and southern Africa in Kampala. One of the WFP's projects in Uganda aims to improve the health of orphans and street children by providing them with meals via the country's many community-based groups and institutions.**

another project to help market vanilla pods. In 2002, the African Development Foundation funded trade and investment projects in Uganda amounting to more than U.S. $1 million.

In 2000, the United States was Uganda's second-largest import partner, after Kenya. In 2002, Uganda's trade with the United States totaled to U.S. $39.3 million. This figure included U.S. $24 million worth of U.S. imports into Uganda and U.S. $15.3 million worth of Ugandan exports to the United States. The value of U.S.-Ugandan trade in the first six months of 2003 reached U.S. $36.4 million.

## Joint Efforts to Combat HIV/AIDS

Uganda and the United States work closely together in the fight against HIV/AIDS. The United States Agency for International Development (USAID) partners with the Ugandan government and local nongovernmental organizations (NGOs) to implement policies to stop the spread of HIV infection in Uganda. The agency is the largest aid group helping Uganda in combating the disease and has donated over U.S. $80 million to the country.

Some USAID initiatives include care for Ugandans living with HIV/AIDS and support for children orphaned by HIV/AIDS. The agency also has supported AIDS education and awareness programs in Uganda. In 2003, the USAID budget to fight HIV/AIDS in Uganda was set at more than U.S. $27 million, which is U.S. $20 million more than in 2002.

*Left:* **U.S. secretary of state Colin Powell (*second from left*) listens to a few Ugandans living with HIV/AIDS tell their stories at Mulago Hospital in Kampala in May 2001. Secretary of State Powell visited Uganda as part of a four-nation tour of the African continent.**

## Americans in Uganda

According to a list compiled in July 1999 by the U.S. Bureau of Consular Affairs, there were about 1,350 Americans living in Kampala, Uganda. This list did not include Americans working for the U.S. government and their families, so the actual number of U.S. citizens living and working in Uganda is likely to be higher. Most Americans in Uganda are there on business, investing in the presently improving economy of Uganda. Other Americans come to Uganda as tourists to enjoy the country's beautiful wildlife. Security at the various national parks is high in order to ensure the safety of the tourists that come from all over the world. The Ugandan embassies in the United States and Canada issue dozens of visas to Americans and Canadians visiting Uganda primarily for tourism. Most North American tourists travel to Uganda with their families.

## Peace Corps Volunteers in Uganda

The U.S. Peace Corps began sending volunteers to Uganda in 1964 and continued to do so until 1973, when the volunteers were withdrawn. The program was reestablished in 1991 but suspended again in 1999. In 2001, volunteers returned to Uganda, with about thirty-five working in the country in 2002 and 2003.

The current group of Peace Corps volunteers in Uganda work as primary-school teacher trainers at teacher-training colleges around the country or as health-care volunteers working with community-based organizations. The teacher trainers help to upgrade the skills of Ugandan teachers and equip them with the know-how to turn their primary schools into community resource centers where programs in health awareness, computer literacy, environmental knowledge, and youth development can be implemented. The health-care volunteers help the Ugandan Ministry of Health to establish and provide home care services and health education, nutrition, and hygiene programs in schools and in the wider community.

## The Carter Center in Uganda

The Carter Center was inaugurated in 1986 at the initiative of former U.S. president Jimmy Carter. Based in Atlanta, Georgia, the Carter Center is a U.S. humanitarian and research institute that has been supporting development and peace projects in Uganda for a number of years. In 2000, the center helped mediate the conflict between the rebels of the Lord's Resistance Army and the Ugandan government. The center also brought together the presidents of Uganda and Sudan to sign an agreement calling for the two countries to respect each other's borders and sovereignty.

*Below:* **Students and a teacher interact at Lincoln International School of Uganda, (LISU) in Kampala. The school provides education for students from pre primary to grade twelve. Offering both U.S. and British-style education, LISU caters to the needs of the international community and counts many U.S. citizens among its staff and student commmunities.**

## Ugandans in North America

The United States is home to many American citizens of Ugandan heritage, as well as immigrants from Uganda. They work in a diverse range of occupations, from teaching, business, and health care to blue-collar jobs and jobs in the arts. Many are Ugandan students pursuing degrees at U.S. universities and colleges. Some of these Ugandan students are excellent sportspeople who have represented their universities and colleges at state and national level competitions. The soccer team of Alabama Agricultural and Mechanical University, for example, has had several talented Ugandan players, including Mujib Kasule, who was the team captain in 2001.

An important association for Ugandans in the United States is the Ugandan North American Association. Founded in 1989 in Atlanta, Georgia, the organization has chapters in various U.S. states as well as in Uganda and other parts of the world. One of the major events organized by the Ugandan North American Association is their annual convention, which draws together Ugandans in the United States, as well as Ugandans from overseas. Over several days, Ugandans and their North American friends interact with each other over meetings, discussions, and cultural events to discuss issues affecting Uganda and the Ugandan community in the United States. The Ugandan North American Association publishes a newsletter and monitors an electronic chat room on the Internet where members can share information and inform others about important issues and events.

### UGANDAN ARTISTS IN THE UNITED STATES

**Some prominent Ugandans living and working in the United States include artists such as James Kitamirike, Fred Makubuya, and Dan Sekanwagi, all of whom have exhibited their work at the Art Room, a gallery in San Francisco that specializes in paintings of East African artists. These artists paint in contemporary styles, and their subjects include Ugandan village life, portraits, and abstract figures. These talented artists also use a variety of media, including oil paint, acrylic paint, dyed cloth, bark cloth, and water colors.**

*Left:* President Yoweri Museveni (*left*) and U.S. secretary of state Colin Powell (*right*) sign Article 98 at the U.S. State Department in Washington, D.C., on June 12, 2003. Article 98 grants to U.S. troops immunity from prosecution by the newly created International Criminal Court in The Hague, in the Netherlands.

*Above:* **North American tourists visit a market in Mbarara, located in southwest Uganda.**

## Relations between Uganda and Canada

Uganda and Canada enjoy warm relations, which mainly focus on trade, development assistance, and regional security issues. Trade between the two nations reaches an average of almost CAN $6 million a year. In 2000, Canada sold to Uganda CAN $3.6 million worth of goods that mostly consisted of chemicals and used clothing. Canada, in turn, imported CAN $1.8 million worth of goods — mainly tea and coffee — from Uganda.

The major Canadian humanitarian organization working in Uganda is the Canadian International Development Agency (CIDA). A Canadian government agency, CIDA has been providing basic health care, clean water, and food to Ugandans affected by the civil war in the north of the country. The organization also helps Ugandan LRA child soldiers recover from the psychological and physical traumas they have experienced. CIDA has spent several million dollars on various other assistance programs to help reduce poverty and disease in Uganda. CIDA also assists the Ugandan government in providing basic education to Ugandan children.

### UGANDAN ASIANS IN CANADA

**Canada accepted over 5,000 South Asians from Uganda in the 1970s, following Idi Amin's expulsion of them in 1972. Most of these Ugandan Asians have become fully integrated into Canadian society. These Ugandan Asians have enriched Canada's culture by contributing toward the country's vibrant multiethnic society. Recently, some of them have returned to Uganda to reclaim land and property.**

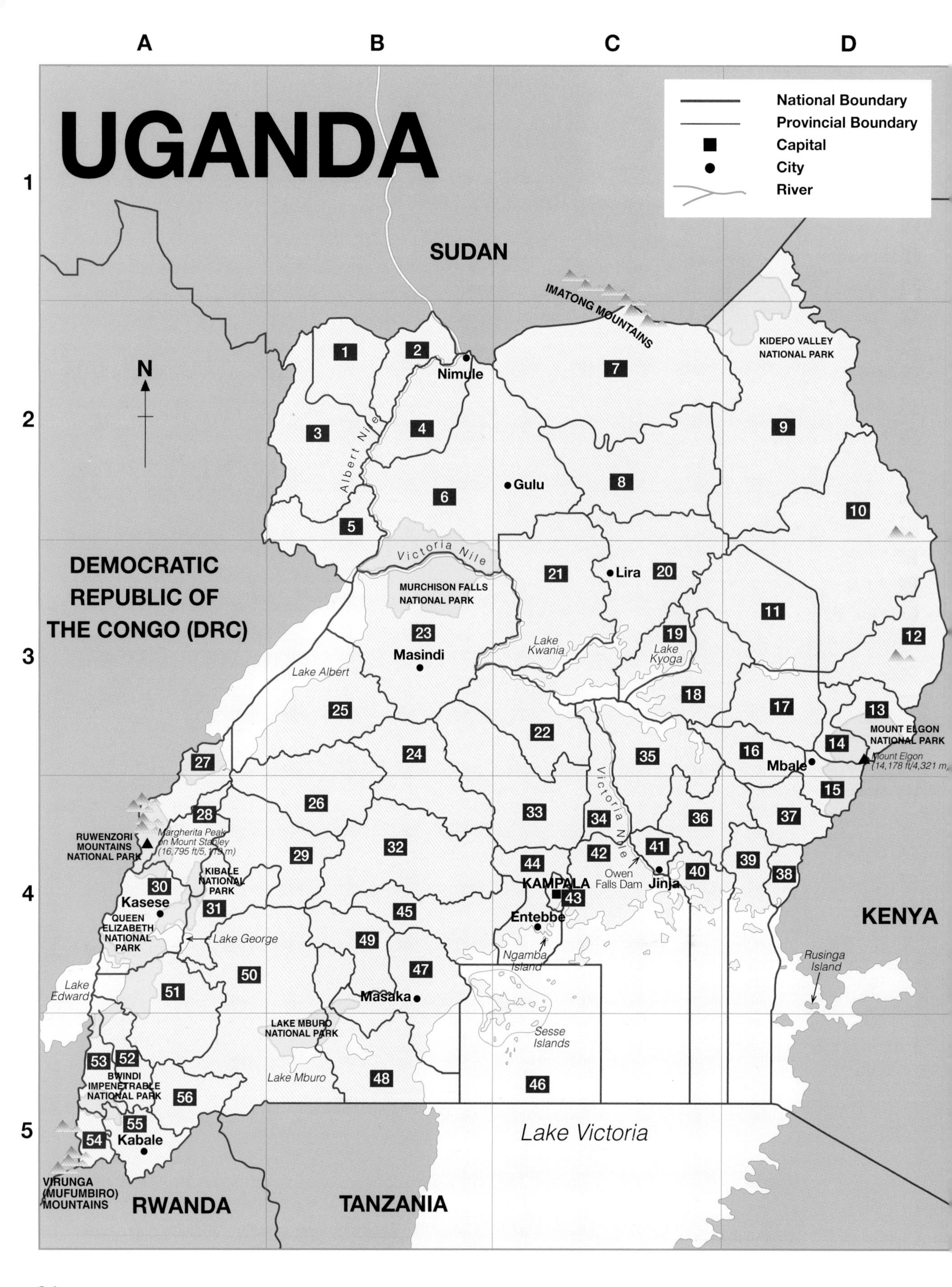
A
B
C
D
1
2
3
4
5
UGANDA
National Boundary
Provincial Boundary
Capital
City
River
SUDAN
IMATONG MOUNTAINS
KIDEPO VALLEY NATIONAL PARK
Nimule
Albert Nile
Gulu
Victoria Nile
DEMOCRATIC REPUBLIC OF THE CONGO (DRC)
MURCHISON FALLS NATIONAL PARK
Lira
Lake Kwania
Lake Kyoga
Masindi
Lake Albert
MOUNT ELGON NATIONAL PARK
Mount Elgon (14,178 ft/4,321 m)
Mbale
Victoria Nile
RUWENZORI MOUNTAINS NATIONAL PARK
Margherita Peak on Mount Stanley (16,795 ft/5,119 m)
KIBALE NATIONAL PARK
Kasese
QUEEN ELIZABETH NATIONAL PARK
Lake George
KAMPALA
Owen Falls Dam
Jinja
Entebbe
Ngamba Island
KENYA
Rusinga Island
Lake Edward
Masaka
Sesse Islands
LAKE MBURO NATIONAL PARK
Lake Mburo
BWINDI IMPENETRABLE NATIONAL PARK
Kabale
Lake Victoria
VIRUNGA (MUFUMBIRO) MOUNTAINS
RWANDA
TANZANIA
1
2
3
4
5
6
7
8
9
10
11
12
13
14
15
16
17
18
19
20
21
22
23
24
25
26
27
28
29
30
31
32
33
34
35
36
37
38
39
40
41
42
43
44
45
46
47
48
49
50
51
52
53
54
55
56

DISTRICTS

1 Yumbe
2 Moyo
3 Arua
4 Adjumani
5 Nebbi
6 Gulu
7 Kitgum
8 Pader
9 Kotido
10 Moroto
11 Katakwi
12 Nakapiripirit
13 Kapchorwa
14 Sironko
15 Mbale
16 Pallisa
17 Kumi
18 Soroti
19 Kaberamaido
20 Lira
21 Apac
22 Nakasongola
23 Masindi
24 Kiboga
25 Hoima
26 Kibale
27 Bundibugyo
28 Kabarole
29 Kyenjojo
30 Kasese
31 Kamwenge
32 Mubende
33 Luwero
34 Kayunga
35 Kamuli
36 Iganga
37 Tororo
38 Busia
39 Bugiri
40 Mayuge
41 Jinja
42 Mukono
43 Kampala
44 Wakiso
45 Mpigi
46 Kalangala
47 Masaka
48 Rakai
49 Sembabule
50 Mbarara
51 Bushenyi
52 Rakungiri
53 Kanungu
54 Kisoro
55 Kabale
56 Ntungamo

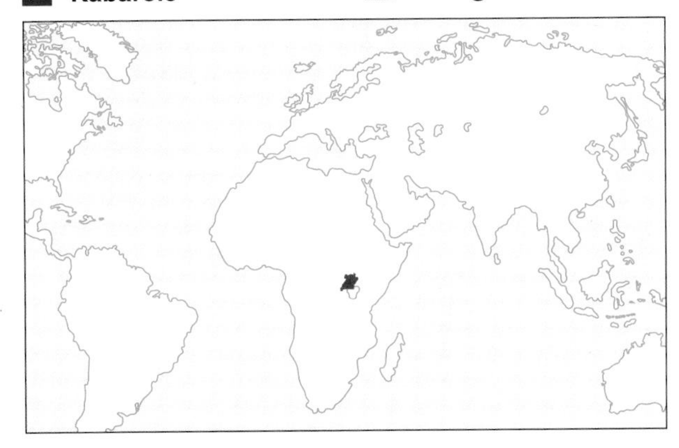

*Above:* Weaving is among the skills taught at this school on Bwama Island in Lake Bunyoni.

Albert Nile B1–B3

Bwindi Impenetrable National Park A5

Democratic Republic of the Congo (DRC) A1–A5

Entebbe C4

Gulu C2

Imatong Mountains C1–C2

Jinja C4

Kabale A5
Kampala C4
Kasese A4
Kenya D1–D5
Kibale National Park A4
Kidepo Valley National Park C2–D1

Lake Albert A3–B3
Lake Edward A4–A5
Lake George A4
Lake Kwania C3
Lake Kyoga C3
Lake Mburo B5
Lake Mburo National Park A5–B4
Lake Victoria B4–D5
Lira C3

Margherita Peak A4
Masaka B4
Masindi B3
Mbale D3
Mount Elgon D3
Mount Elgon National Park D3–D4
Mount Stanley A4
Murchison Falls National Park B2–C3

Ngamba Island C4
Nimule B2

Owen Falls Dam C4

Queen Elizabeth National Park A4–A5

Rusinga Island D4
Ruwenzori Mountains National Park A4
Rwanda A5–B5

Sesse Islands B4–C5
Sudan A1–D1

Tanzania A5–D5

Victoria Nile B3–C4
Virunga (Mufumbiro) Mountains A5

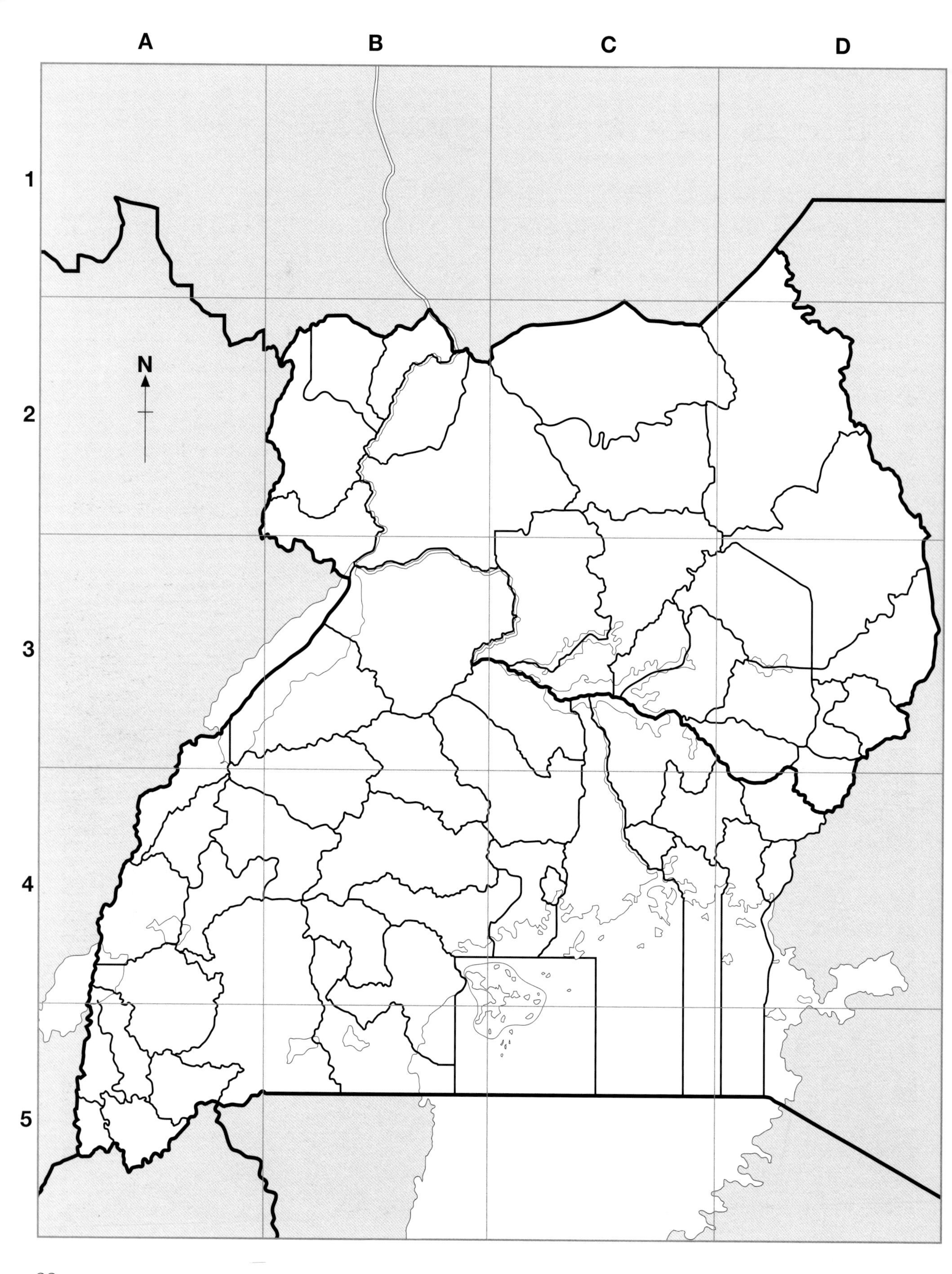
A
B
C
D
1
2
3
4
5
N

# How Is Your Geography?

Learning to identify the main geographical areas and points of a country can be challenging. Although it may seem difficult at first to memorize the locations and spellings of major cities or the names of mountain ranges, rivers, deserts, lakes, and other prominent physical features, the end result of this effort can be very rewarding. Places you previously did not know existed will suddenly come to life when referred to in world news, whether in newspapers, television reports, other books and reference sources, or on the Internet. This knowledge will make you feel a bit closer to the rest of the world, with its fascinating variety of cultures and physical geography.

This map can be duplicated for use in a classroom. (PLEASE DO NOT WRITE IN THIS BOOK!) Students can then fill in any requested information on their individual map copies. The student can also make a copy of the map and use it as a study tool to practice identifying place names and geographical features on his or her own.

***Above:*** **Two Baganda men hold up a piece of cloth made from tree bark.**

# Uganda at a Glance

| | |
|---|---|
| **Official Name** | Republic of Uganda |
| **Capital** | Kampala |
| **Land Area** | 91,111 square miles (236,040 square kilometers) |
| **Administrative divisions** | Adjumani, Apac, Arua, Bugiri, Bundibugyo, Bushenyi, Busia, Gulu, Hoima, Iganga, Jinja, Kabale, Kabarole, Kaberamaido, Kalangala, Kampala, Kamuli, Kamwenge, Kanungu, Kapchorwa, Kasese, Katakwi, Kayunga, Kibale, Kiboga, Kisoro, Kitgum, Kotido, Kumi, Kyenjojo, Lira, Luwero, Masaka, Masindi, Mayuge, Mbale, Mbarara, Moroto, Moyo, Mpigi, Mubende, Mukono, Nakapiripirit, Nakasongola, Nebbi, Ntungamo, Pader, Pallisa, Rakai, Rukungiri, Sembabule, Sironko, Soroti, Tororo, Wakiso, Yumbe |
| **Population** | 25,632,794 (July 2003 estimate) |
| **Highest Point** | Margherita Peak 16,795 feet (5,119 m) |
| **Major Rivers** | Victoria Nile, Albert Nile |
| **Official Language** | English |
| **Major Religions** | Protestantism, Roman Catholicism, Islam, Indigenous beliefs |
| **Famous Leaders** | Milton Obote (1924– )<br>Idi Amin (1925–2003)<br>Yoweri Museveni (1944– )<br>Dr. Specioza Wandira (1955– ) |
| **Important Holidays** | New Year's Day, *Eid al-Adha*, Martyrs's Day, Independence Day, *Eid al-Fitr*, Christmas Day, Boxing Day |
| **Major Exports** | Coffee, frozen fish, tea, gold, cotton, flowers |
| **Major Imports** | Vehicles, petroleum, medical supplies, cereals |
| **Currency** | (1,986 UGX = U.S. $1 as of August 2003) |

***Opposite:*** **The batik-style painting is by Nuwa Wamala Nnyanzi, an accomplished Ugandan artist.**

# Glossary

## Ugandan Vocabulary

***akadinda*** **(AH-kah-din-dah):** a type of xylophone that usually has either ten or twenty relatively small keys.

***amadinda*** **(AH-mah-din-dah):** a type of xylophone that usually has fifteen keys.

***amagunju*** **(AH-MAH-gun-joo):** a traditional dance of the Baganda people.

***bafaransa*** **(BUH-fah-rah-sah):** a Luganda term meaning "the French" that traditionally referred to Roman Catholic Christian missionaries.

***balokole*** **(BAH-loh-koh-lee):** a Luganda term meaning "born again."

***bangerezza*** **(BUNG-guh-ree-zah):** a Luganda term meaning "the British" that traditionally referred to the Protestant Christian missionaries.

***busuti*** **(BOO-su-tih):** a traditional, long dress worn by Soga women.

***Cwezi*** **(SEE-wee-ze):** the early kingdoms of the Bantu-speaking peoples.

***gombolola*** **(gohm-boh-LOH-lah):** a county court.

***kabaka*** **(KAH-baa-kah):** a king of Buganda.

***kanzu*** **(KAHN-zoo):** a traditional, white robe worn by Soga men.

***luwombo*** **(lu-WOM-boh):** a steamed mixture of meat and vegetables wrapped in banana leaves.

***matooke*** **(maa-TOO-kee):** plantains that taste like potatoes when cooked.

***Mkate mayai*** **(UHM-kah-tee MAH-yah-ee):** a popular snack in Uganda made of mincemeat and egg wrapped in a thin pancake.

***Muntu*** **(MOON-too):** a god in which some Bantu-speaking peoples believe.

***Ntu*** **(UN-too):** another name for Muntu.

***pombe*** **(POM-bee):** banana beer.

***omweso*** **(OM-wee-soh):** a Ugandan board game that involves strategy and mathematical skill.

***ugali*** **(oo-GAAH-lee):** a type of corn bread.

***waragi*** **(WAH-raa-gee):** an alcoholic beverage made from millet.

## English Vocabulary

**abstain:** to voluntarily avoid an object or action.

**affiliation:** association or connection.

**aides:** assistants.

**alliances:** an agreement between two or more persons or organizations made to further shared interests.

**animistic:** believing that natural objects, natural phenomena, and the universe itself possess souls.

**armor:** any covering worn as a defense against weapons.

**autonomy:** the right or ability of self-government.

**beatified:** in Christianity, given a religious honor for deceased persons thought to be blessed by Heaven.

**beheaded:** having had one's head cut off; decapitated.

**biodiversity:** the variety of plant and animal species in an environment.

**Commonwealth:** a group of countries and their territories united by historical ties to the British Empire; countries in the group cooperate on matters of shared concern.

**canonized:** officially declared a saint.

**cassava:** a type of root vegetable; also known as tapioca.

**curriculum:** the range of subjects offered in a school or college.

**disarray:** disorder and confusion.

**doctorate:** a degree of the highest rank offered by a university.

**doctrines:** teachings; ideas taught as principles of a religion.

**elusive:** escaping one's clear perception; difficult to identify.

**etched:** fixed or imprinted firmly.

**expelled:** driven or forced out.

**exploitable:** able to be harvested or utilized for profit.

**federal:** part of a union of states that is controlled by a central government that is separate from the individual governments that control each state.

**genome:** total genetic composition.

**governance:** method or system of government or management of authority.

**guerrilla:** specializing in raids and sabotage against the dominant power.

**impenetrable:** impossible to penetrate.

**innovation:** the introduction of something new.

**landlocked:** completely surrounded by land.

**legitimacy:** rightfulness or lawfulness.

**massifs:** masses of rock that are parts of Earth's crust that have been pushed upward by immense moving forces originating beneath the crust.

**martyrs:** persons who are willing to suffer death rather than renounce their beliefs.

**Mecca:** a city in western Saudi Arabia; the spiritual center of Islam.

**mythical:** having the characteristics of a myth.

**nuclear:** when describing a family, consisting of a husband, wife, and their children.

**nullified:** cancelled.

**ornithologists:** people who scientifically study birds.

**ousted:** expelled or removed from the position occupied.

**pilgrimage:** a long journey to a sacred place that believers of a particular religion make to show their devotion.

**plumage:** the entire feathery covering of a bird.

**polygamy:** the practice of having more than one wife.

**protectorate:** a weaker state or territory that is protected and partly controlled by a stronger state.

**reinforce:** strengthen or support.

**sovereignty:** supreme power of a ruler over a country or people.

**statuesque:** resembling a statue in beauty and grace.

**steward:** a person in charge of running the household of another.

**submerged:** covered by water.

**thatch:** a covering made from leaves, straw, or other similar materials.

**tyrannical:** oppressive; unjustly cruel or severe.

**unicameral:** having a single legislative body.

**usurped:** seized unlawfully or by force.

# More Books to Read

*Abayudaya: The Jews of Uganda.* Richard Sobol (Abbeville Press)

*East Africa. Country Fact Files* series. Rob Bowden (Raintree/Steck Vaughan)

*Gorillas in the Mist.* Dian Fossey (Mariner Books)

*Uganda. Cultures of the World* series. Robert Barlas (Marshall Cavendish)

*Uganda. Enchantment of the World* series. Ettagale Blauer (Children's Press)

*Uganda. Major World Nations* series. Alexander Creed (Chelsea House)

*Uganda. Oxfam Country Profiles* series. Ian Leggett (Oxfam Publications)

# Videos

*East Africa. Worlds Together* series. (Elmer Hawkes)

*Gorillas in the Mist.* (Universal Studios)

*Travel the World by Train: Africa — Morocco, Tunisia, Egypt, Kenya, Uganda, South Africa.* (Pioneer)

*Trekking in Uganda and Congo.* (Lonely Planet)

*Uganda: Wildlife on the Edge. Investigative Reports Science* series. (A & E Home Video)

# Web Sites

allafrica.com/uganda/

www.buganda.com

www.government.go.ug/

www.sas.upenn.edu/African_Studies/Country_Specific/Uganda.html

www.wougnet.org/

Due to the dynamic nature of the Internet, some web sites stay current longer than others. To find additional web sites, use a reliable search engine with one or more of the following keywords to help you locate information about Uganda. Keywords: *Idi Amin, Jinja, Kampala, Lake Victoria, mountain gorillas, Yoweri Museveni, Victoria Nile.*

# Index